# Wicked
# NEW ALBANY

# Wicked
# NEW ALBANY

GREGG
SEIDL

Charleston · London

THE
History
PRESS

Published by The History Press
Charleston, SC 29403
www.historypress.net

Images are courtesy of the author unless otherwise noted.

*Cover image*: Map of New Albany is from the *Illustrated Historical Atlas of the State of Indiana*, by Baskin, Forester & Co., produced in 1876. *Courtesy of the Indiana Room*.

First published 2011
Manufactured in the United States

ISBN 978.1.60949.462.9

Library of Congress Cataloging-in-Publication Data

Seidl, Gregg.
Wicked New Albany / Gregg Seidl.
p. cm.
ISBN 978-1-60949-462-9
1. New Albany (Ind.)--History--Anecdotes. 2. Crime--Indiana--New Albany--History--Anecdotes. 3. Corruption--Indiana--New Albany--History--Anecdotes. 4. New Albany (Ind.)--Social conditions--Anecdotes. 5. New Albany (Ind.)--Biography--Anecdotes. I. Title.
F534.N4S46 2011
977.2'19--dc23
2011036373

*Notice*: The information in this book is true and complete to the best of our knowledge. It is offered without guarantee on the part of the author or The History Press. The author and The History Press disclaim all liability in connection with the use of this book.

*To my great-grandmother Mary Bell, née Thomas Fothergill,*

*a grand old lady of the Victorian era*

*and my first experience with the dead*

*Men fear death as children fear to go in the dark; and as that natural fear in children is increased by tales, so is the other.*

*—Francis Bacon*

# Contents

Acknowledgements     11

Introduction     13

**PART I. MURDER MOST FOUL**     **17**

Sullivan Subdivided     18

In Exordium     19

The Cup That Poisons the Soul     23

The "Happy Home Converted into a Hell by the Demon Whisky"     35

It Was a Dark and Stormy Night—Really!     46

Mommy Dearest     54

**PART II. THE STEEL WHEELS OF DEATH**     **83**

A Family Torn to Pieces     84

Under the Wheels     88

The Engine of Death     91

Death of the Dinky Man     94

Cut to Pieces     97

**PART III. SUICIDES**     **99**

"I Dread the Night in This Gloomy Building"     101

"A Very Unpleasant and Painful Act"     103

# Contents

Mrs. Manor's Self-Murder            107

A Horrible Sight                    109

If Only He Hadn't Kicked the Bucket 111

Tragedy on Thanksgiving Day         113

Care to Make a Bet?                 119


Notes                               139

About the Author                    141

# Acknowledgements

Seldom do we create anything without the assistance of others. This collection of gruesome and untimely deaths in my hometown of New Albany, Indiana, is no exception.

My thanks go out to Jason Kingsley, and his staff at the Fairview Cemetery, for granting me access to his vast knowledge of the burial ground, as well as for helping maintain this important piece of the city's history. Thanks to Lisa Wepf for exploring the third floor of her business with me; and to Melissa and Gary Humphrey, owners of the River City Winery; Leo Lopez, owner of the Habana Blues Tapas Restaurant; Roger Baylor, owner of the New Albanian Brewing Company; Matt McMahan, owner of The Irish Exit; and Hugh E. Bir, owner of the world-famous Hugh E. Bir's Café, New Albany's original "Fourth Street Live," for granting me access to their respective businesses.

Thanks are in order to the staff of the Indiana Room in the New Albany/Floyd County Library. Without their help and guidance, this book would not have been possible. Several historians, both professional and amateur, provided me with a wealth of information, and I'd like to acknowledge the work of Floyd County historians David Barksdale, Beth Nolan, Barbara Adams Whiteside, Barbara Ann Guyton Ziegenmeyer and Sue Carpenter. Their dedication to preserving New Albany's history saved me hours of research, and the eagle eye of Melissa Lutz improved a substandard manuscript.

I'd like to extend my appreciation to New Albany police chief Todd Bailey, chief of detectives Keith Whitlow, detective Perry Parsons and retired chief of detectives Mike Culwell for sharing their knowledge with me. I'd also like to extend my deepest gratitude to the men and women of the department, both past and present, for the hard work and sacrifices they and their families made and continue to make in their efforts to keep our city safe.

Shirley Schultz, Nancy Falkenstein, Paul Gibson, Ken Stutsman, Jerry Rodgers, Tresa Reynolds, and Dr. William Sweigart shaped and encouraged my writing. Without them, this book would never have happened.

A special thank you is in order to Dr. Glenn Crothers, Dr. Frank Thackeray and, most importantly, Dr. John Findling for their tolerance and direction teaching me the historian's craft. I'm not dodging spitballs yet, John, and my debt to you still stands.

I'd like express my gratitude to my editor at The History Press, Joseph Gartrell, for his patience and guidance in putting this work together. The entire staff at The History Press has been most helpful and made this a rewarding and enjoyable experience.

My daughter, Amy Seidl, always supported me, and I'd like to publicly express my most sincere gratitude to her for being such a wonderful daughter. Daddy loves you, Bo.

Finally, my deepest appreciation goes to my assistant/confidant/in-house editor—my beautifully talented wife, Corine Seidl. Without the talents and support of the "Grammar Queen," I'd be nothing. KAF.

My sincere apologies to anyone I may have inadvertently omitted.

# Introduction

Every town has those dark places where the foulest of felonies once occurred, deeds so despicable that most people prefer to forget they ever happened, and even those not so willing—or unable—to forget the grisly proceedings generally speak of the horrible events in hushed whispers behind closed doors with only their most trusted and closest associates.

My hometown of New Albany, Indiana, is no exception.

Death is commonly defined as the cessation of the biological actions necessary to sustain life. Relatively few people throughout human history knew prior to the event exactly the moment when they would cease to exist as a living, breathing human being. The terminally ill, while aware their end is rapidly approaching, seldom know the precise time or day when they will lose their battle. Other folks grow aware of their imminent death only in the brief few moments directly preceding their demise—passengers on out-of-control airplanes; soldiers crossing open fields under enemy fire; auto accident victims in the moment they lose control of their vehicles; murder victims in the seconds before their assailant pulls the trigger or slashes with a knife, or as their vision slowly fades to black as they are slowly choked to death.

Suicide victims, depending on the method they choose to make their exit, can also usually know roughly when they will meet their ends. If they use a firearm, as so many typically do, or if they place a noose around their necks and spend their last few agonizing moments struggling to draw one last breath, these people can make a fairly accurate estimate of their departure from this earthly plane. Those who opt to open the veins and arteries in their wrists—or their throats—can also often predict within a few minutes when they will expire; sometimes, but as seen in one gruesome case depicted in this book, not always.

Those who elect an exit through poison or sleeping pills can't quite get as close to an accurate departure time, nor can those who sit in a running automobile in a closed garage predict the exact moment when death will free them from their tortured existence.

For most of us, death usually comes like the proverbial thief in the night—unannounced and unexpected—the manner in which we will die as unknown to us as the precise moment in which we will pass. The methods by which we will lose our lives are as many as the stars in the heavens, and lucky indeed is the person who faces this inevitable end after a long and well-lived life, safe and comfortable in his bed, surrounded by grieving friends and loved ones. Unfortunately, far more of us will meet an unexpected and violent end than will pass peacefully at home.

We will die in industrial accidents, our mangled remains a challenge for the funeral home workers who work to make our mutilated corpses presentable for our loved ones. Though the technicians often succeed in their macabre art, many of us will be left in such terrible states that an open casket is out of the question. Some of us will be brutally murdered when an axe or hammer splits open our skulls, our cracked craniums oozing grayish, sticky gobs on the pavement. Others will fight futilely against an attacker armed with a sharp knife or an ice pick as our blood sprays in hot streams that pool in sticky crimson ponds as our assailant slashes and jabs with his sharp, pointy instruments. Many of us will simply cease to exist when an unseen assailant squeezes the trigger and splatters shattered little bits of our skull, brain and flesh in patterns that resemble some gruesome abstract painting on the walls of the homes where we once felt so safe and secure.

Industrial fatalities, suicides and murders are the main topics covered in this book. I have chosen not to include deaths from automobile accidents simply because there are so many of them that they would and could be another book entirely, and with rare exceptions, most such deaths are not as "spectacular" and do not create quite the sensation among the general public as the aforementioned endings.

I have included a section on deaths generated when human flesh meets the steel wheels of a passing train, but only because such deaths are generally gruesome, and I assume that if you've bought this book, gruesome is what you seek!

I have left out any stories of deaths that occurred within the last ten years out of respect to the surviving family members of the victims, as well as members of the perpetrators' families. I have omitted two cases that, while certainly falling in the category of "sensational," didn't occur within the city limits of present-day New Albany. The murders of Kim Camm and her five-year-old daughter, Jill, and seven year-old son, Brad, allegedly committed by Kim's husband, former Indiana State Police trooper David Camm,[1] have been excluded because, while they occurred in Floyd County, they happened in Georgetown and not in New Albany. Similarly, the murder of thirteen-year-old Shanda Sharer is absent from these pages. Though the case meets my criteria for gruesome death, Shanda, abducted from her home in New Albany and brutally tortured for hours by four other teenage girls during the late-night hours of January 10, 1992, died outside Madison, Indiana, when her tormentors set the partially conscious teen's badly beaten body on fire shortly before daybreak on January 11, 1992.

NATIVE AMERICANS FIRST inhabited the area that became New Albany, Indiana. Bands of the aborigines stopped in the area on the journey between their winter and summer camps, and the archaeological evidence shows us that humans have walked this land for the past ten thousand years. During this period, murders and other forms of violent, unnatural death certainly occurred, but no account exists today documenting these deaths. Local legend does, however, mention at least two such deaths, which I discuss in this book.

The first recorded whites to settle the area, French immigrants, mostly former soldiers in Napoleon's army and their families, squatted with no legal claim to the land upon which they built their rough log cabins. Revolutionary War hero George Rogers Clark, awarded a large tract of land north of the Ohio River that included the future site of New Albany for his services during the war, sold some of his grant to former comrades and rewarded others with gifts of land for their services to him during the war. Colonel John Paul's gifted tract included the upcoming town.

Nestled between hardwood-covered hills and the northern bank of the Ohio River on the downriver end of the Falls of the Ohio, the area attracted the attention of three brothers from New York State. Abner, Joel and Nathaniel Scribner correctly believed that the area's location and abundant natural resources meant prosperity for any city situated on the site. They bought the land from Colonel Paul in 1812 for the princely sum of ten dollars an acre, five times the going rate for undeveloped frontier land. They envisioned their new town as the future head of downriver navigation and named their city New Albany in honor of the capital of their home state. In 1817, the year after Indiana attained statehood, their town was incorporated as part of Clark County, but on March 4, 1819, state officials created Floyd County out of Clark and Harrison Counties and made the Scribner's town the county seat. Despite some initial difficulties, the town quickly lived up to the brothers' expectations and soon became Indiana's largest, most powerful city, a distinction the town held until late in the nineteenth century.

New Albany is generally a quiet, peaceful little town, and the city's residents enjoy a relatively calm life, generally free from the worries of big city living. However, on occasion, madness and misfortune stalked New Albany's usually serene streets, and I hope you enjoy these stories of disasters and calamities. Let the tales I share with you serve as a warning that death comes in any one of a number of horrific ways and often when least expected. Live your life as if every day is your last, for one *will* be your last. Always let your loved ones know how much you appreciate them. We never know when we walk out our doors if the parting will be the last time we gaze upon their loving faces in this earthly existence.

Most of the places I have written about belong to private individuals who aren't at all interested in letting you into their homes or on their property and likely won't want to talk to you about what happened. Most probably aren't aware of what occurred until the release of this book. They aren't responsible for what happened and are entitled to their privacy. If you insist on visiting these sites, please be respectful of their right to privacy, as well as that of their neighbors.

Most importantly, be careful. Bad things have happened in these locations, and if evil exists, who knows what lurks in the places where madness and insanity once ruled—even if only briefly!

# Part I

# Murder Most Foul

*Each murder is one too many.*
*—Jurgen Habermas*

The Federal Bureau of Investigation's Uniform Crime Reporting Program (UCR) defines murder and non-negligent manslaughter as the willful (non-negligent) killing of one human being by another. The UCR claims a homicide occurs approximately every thirty-five minutes in the United States.

More than 15,000 murders[2] occurred in this country in 2009, the last year for available statistics at the time of this writing. Firearms of all kinds, from handguns to rifles to shotguns, killed more than 9,000 Americans that year. Cutting, slashing and/or hacking accounted for approximately another 1,800 of us. Around 860 died at the hands and/or feet of their assailants. The rest met their ends in a variety of nasty little encounters and a wide range of methods, and 5 out of every 100,000 Americans died at the hands of a killer in 2009. California, with 1,972 victims, had the highest number of murders that year. Texas followed close behind, with 1,325 homicides, and Vermont's 7 killings ranked the state as the nation's lowest in 2009 for homicides.

Approximately 293 homicides occurred in Indiana in 2009, most by some type of firearm. New Albany's only murder that year happened when forty-two-year-old Freddie Love of Louisville, Kentucky, shot and killed his co-worker, forty-eight-year-old Christopher J. Trowell, also of Louisville, in the parking lot of the Pillsbury plant on Grantline Road in New Albany on Wednesday, August 6. Both men worked in the plant, and Love allegedly killed his co-worker over a domestic dispute involving Trowell and the killer's wife.[3]

The city stayed relatively peaceful that year, but serenity hasn't always been the case in New Albany. Throughout the city's almost two-hundred-year history, friends murdered friends, wives killed husbands, husbands slaughtered wives, sons and daughters killed mothers and fathers and parents slayed children. Some of the homicides were premeditated and well planned; others were heat-of-the-moment crimes of passion.

Some killers forfeited their own lives for their crimes, but others carried out their dastardly plans so skillfully that they never faced any earthly retribution. Most of those who escaped official retribution did so through sheer luck, but some walked free after only a short time behind bars when a jury of their peers found their murderous actions justifiable, and on more than one occasion, a killer sentenced to a long stretch behind bars went free due to technicalities after serving only a fraction of his sentence.

This chapter deals with some of the more notorious homicides in our usually tranquil town. I haven't included all of the city's murders—such an account would likely fill several volumes, but I think you'll find the stories I include interesting and sufficiently ghastly to suit your desire for gruesome and grisly tales. I hope you enjoy the accounts regarding the murderous mayhem that sometimes takes place in my generally pleasant and peaceful town.

When you're done, ya'll come on back, now. Ya heah?

## SULLIVAN SUBDIVIDED

A grand old building once stood on the southwest corner of Spring and Pearl Streets in downtown New Albany. The massive stone structure housed the United States Customs and Post Office until the mid-1960s, when the city's leaders razed the fortress-like structure and replaced it with a parking lot. Before the post office occupied the space, homes and businesses stood on the corner, all removed in the name of progress.

Before the buildings that rose and then fell on this site, a salt lick once occupied the space. Salt licks are good ambush sites. Hunters find sneaking up on their normally wary quarry easier when the animal's attention is temporarily distracted, and many a critter ended up in the hungry bellies of those patient enough to wait for their prey to drop their heads and start licking from the ground the minerals necessary to the animals' survival.

For experienced hunters, two-legged prey is sometimes even easier to take than the four-legged variety. On a warm fall day a few years before the Scribners arrived, a passing band of local braves waylaid an unfortunate young white immigrant named Sullivan. There's no official record of whether this is his first name or his last, and the only thing that remains of the man is the story of his gruesome demise.

Not long after nabbing their captive, the natives cut Sullivan into four separate pieces and then buried the four bloody chunks according to the points of their compass. I assume they killed Sullivan before they carved him up, but that's only an assumption. They may well have cut him in four sections while he was alive and completely aware of every hack made on his person.

We know about Sullivan's quartering because one of his executioners converted to Christianity several years later and confessed the crime to the horror of the priest who heard the admission.

Sullivan wasn't the first settler killed by young native men, nor did he suffer the most savage ending meted out along the banks of the Ohio by young braves on a young white man. The killing wasn't the worst death inflicted on a young native by a group of young white men, nor was Sullivan's the ghastliest ending for a woman or a child of either ethnicity. Murder—murder most foul—most of it unreported, was common for hundreds, if not thousands, of years. Hundreds more have been reported since the area became "civilized."

# In Exordium

Two unnamed men spent a beautiful spring morning in 1820 checking their trotlines, heavy lines rigged with hooks and bait at regular intervals, for any fish or turtles hooked during the previous night in the Ohio River below the rapidly growing town of New Albany. They'd put a number of fish in their little skiff when they pulled up a large bag snared on one of the sharp hooks. The pair pulled the heavy sack out of the river, and when one of them slit the cloth with his pocketknife, a foul stench flooded the air. The men retched and covered their noses and mouths against the disgusting odor as they poked at the contents inside.

Lying amid a collection of old pots, pans and skillets in the bag, they were horrified to see the rotting remains of a man. They quickly rowed their little boat to the shore and notified the authorities, who, after a brief examination of the waterlogged corpse, identified the body as that of Frederick Nolte, an emigrant from Germany. Nolte, who operated a bakery from his log home on the southeast corner of Pearl and Main Streets, had unexpectedly disappeared about a week before the fishermen discovered his bagged and bloated body.

Due to the city's location on the downriver end of the falls of the Ohio River, people arrived in and departed from New Albany on a regular basis. Some stayed only a few hours. Others stayed for days, weeks, months or even years before one day deciding to move on farther down the river, and no one had seriously questioned Nolte's sudden departure; at least, not until the discovery of his decomposing corpse. The large slash across the victim's throat spoke volumes about how he'd met his demise, and suspicion immediately turned to John Dahmen, a recent Danish immigrant to the area. Dahmen lived on a farm about thirty miles downriver from New Albany and often stayed in Nolte's little cabin when visiting the town.

Though New Albany eventually grew into Indiana's largest, most economically powerful city, the population of the town remained small in 1820, and like in small towns everywhere, everybody knew everyone else and their "business." Many of the town's residents knew that on the night before his unexpected departure, Nolte spent the evening drinking with Dahmen. Several witnesses saw the drunken Dane leaving the city sometime in the early morning hours of the day his drinking partner unexpectedly left New Albany. Three days after Nolte disappeared, Dahmen returned to the city, claiming that Nolte had sold him the bakery before leaving the city. No one questioned his claim, and Dahmen quickly sold the building and its contents before returning to his farm.

Floyd County sheriff James Besse set out for Dahmen's farm and, three days later, arrested the murderous immigrant working in the fields around his home. According to Sherriff Besse's later testimony, Dahmen didn't appear too concerned about the arrest. Besse returned to New Albany with his prisoner and placed him in the recently built Floyd County Jail, a log structure built for the princely sum of fifty dollars. Though fifty dollars bought way more in 1820 than the same amount does today, it obviously didn't buy much security. Not long after his confinement, Dahmen bored a hole in the wood floor, tunneled his way out and headed to Canada.

Unable to contact her the night of his escape, he had reluctantly left his beloved wife in New Albany. He missed her greatly and not long after getting settled in his new home wrote her a letter detailing his location and asking her to join him. He wrote the letter in Norwegian, apparently in the belief that if anyone intercepted the message, they'd be unable to decipher the contents. Why he assumed his wife read the language we'll probably never know, but unfortunately for Dahmen, she didn't. She asked a neighbor, a man known to us today simply as Hawkins, to translate the letter. Hawkins read the letter to her and then promptly reported the contents of the message to Sheriff Besse.

Besse, determined to bring the killer to justice, enlisted the aid of New Albany resident and merchant John Eastman, and the pair set out to return Dahmen to New Albany. Their journey north took almost five weeks. Once they arrived, they quickly located the house where Dahmen boarded, and Besse, not wanting to deal with all of the paperwork required for the formal removal of his quarry, devised a plan to avoid the legalities.

Besse had Eastman dress in women's clothing, and the pair went to the home. Besse told the landlord that Dahmen's heart-broken wife wished to see her husband as soon as possible. When Dahmen rushed to meet his beloved, he quickly found himself subdued, handcuffed and on his way back to New Albany. The trio made their way to Pittsburgh, Pennsylvania, and from there traveled by flatboat down the Ohio River to New Albany. The return trip took only about two weeks on the fast-moving waters.

In December 1820, the grand jury indicted Dahmen for the murder of Frederick Nolte. The trial, held in the basement of the First Presbyterian Church on State Street, began in May 1821. Though Dahmen denied that he'd murdered Nolte, and his lawyer asked for a new trial when the prisoner explained how he'd come to be in the court, the jury didn't deliberate long before returning a guilty verdict.

On May 19, Judge David Floyd pronounced the sentence:

*The motion for a new trial heretofore entered in this case is overruled. It is therefore considered by the court, that the said John Dahmen be taken to the jail of said county, from whence he came, and from thence to the place of execution on the 6th day of July, 1821, between the hours of 12 and 4 o'clock of said day, and there be hanged by the neck until he be dead, dead, dead.*

Dahmen showed surprisingly little emotion when he heard the sentence pronounced. When Judge Floyd added, "And may God have mercy on your soul," Dahmen shocked those present in the courtroom when he responded, "Yes, and the Devil, too." The convicted man then surprisingly confessed that he had indeed murdered Nolte.

Dahmen claimed he had spent several hours drinking with his victim when the idea suddenly popped into his head to murder and rob the baker, and when he got the chance, he hit Nolte in the head with a club, rendering him unconscious. Dahmen then removed some of the floorboards, dug a shallow hole in the ground underneath, dragged Nolte's body to the hole and cut the baker's throat, making sure the torrent of hot blood drained into the dirt. He didn't want any stains on the floorboards. He told the stunned crowd he had replaced the dirt in the hole, put the floorboards back in place and then put Nolte's lifeless body in the dead man's bed tick, along with several pots, pans and skillets, before sewing shut the bag and its grisly contents. He put his ghastly package on a wide board to ease in transporting the improvised body bag the short distance down to the river, where he put his dreadful load in a small skiff, rowed to the middle of the river and watched as the nasty little container slowly sank from sight. The killer then told the astonished crowd that the night he'd killed his drinking partner wasn't the first time he'd suddenly felt an irresistible urge to kill. He boasted to his horrified listeners that he'd murdered so many people on impulse that he'd long ago lost count of his victims.

Between the sentencing and the actual execution, Dahmen sold his body to Dr. Asahel Clapp, New Albany's first physician. Once he got Clapp's money, Dahmen tried to annul the contract and have his corpse put up for sale at public auction after the execution to the highest bidder. The battle for the body continued up to the day of his execution on July 6, 1821.

The hanging took place near what is today the drive-through of the PNC Bank on the northeast corner of State and Spring Streets in downtown New Albany. Dahmen showed no emotion as he rode to the site in the back of a light wagon. He adamantly refused to have any clergy near him, claiming—as he'd done since his conviction—that Satan, his father, wouldn't approve. Sherriff Besse preceded his prisoner to the scaffold, described as a "plain affair with a trap door suspended with a figure four trigger." Asked by Besse if he had any last words, Dahmen shook his head no. The sheriff placed a black hood over the prisoner's head, placed and properly adjusted the noose around the condemned's neck, then walked to the side of the small platform and immediately released the trap without hesitation. Dahmen's body dropped about four feet, his neck broke cleanly and the unrepentant killer died almost instantly.

Approximately twenty minutes later, Besse removed the corpse, putting the dead man in the back of the same wagon that had brought Dahmen to the site of his execution. The record is unclear here as to where Besse delivered the body. One source claims Dr. Clapp dissected the body somewhere in the old Southside Building on Main Street. Another account claims Dr. Strickland dissected the corpse in his office on Water Street.

According to an account in the *New Albany Daily Ledger Standard* written almost sixty years after the event, New Albany's first public hanging generated "a general feeling among the public after his death that it was a righteous execution."

## THE CUP THAT POISONS THE SOUL

On April 6 and 7, 1862, more than 100,000 men met near the western shore of the Tennessee River in southwestern Tennessee. Two days later, more than 23,000 lay dead in the fields and woods surrounding the river. The horrific struggle that occurred over those two days (known as the Battle of Shiloh if you study northern accounts of the fight and as the Battle of Pittsburgh Landing if you study southern histories of the conflict), the deadliest battle of the American Civil War at the time it occurred, showed both sides that the war would be neither as short nor as easy as either side originally thought. The warfare that took place on those two spring days constitutes the ninth deadliest battle of the war, but the battle continued killing long after the fighting ended, sometimes miles away from the bloodied ground where the mêlée occurred.

Hundreds of volunteers from New Albany fought at Shiloh. Two of those volunteers, Thomas P. Moore, a native of New Albany and a sergeant in Company E of the Twenty-third Indiana Volunteer Infantry regiment, and Thomas Krementz, a native of Germany and a lieutenant in Company A of the Twenty-third, fought side by side at some point in the battle. Their fellow New Albanians so highly regarded both men that when the Twenty-third "mustered into" service of the Federal government in late July 1861 at Camp Noble in New Albany, their comrades elected them to their respective ranks. Not long after the war ended in April 1865, the pair "mustered out" of service and returned to New Albany.

Not long after his return, Moore, the son of Thomas Moore, a representative from the Harrodsburg district in Kentucky to the United States House of Representatives for many years, married Elizabeth Emily Gwin, a highly respected young lady from New Albany. By the summer of 1868, the pair, with their newborn son, Harry, had settled into a small home located next to her father's stables on Market Street, close to East Third Street. Krementz, who married Mary Meyers after his return, worked as a bartender in Belvidere's Saloon across the street from where the Moores resided on her father's property. Thomas often spent his leisure hours in the saloon.

On Monday, July 27, 1868, a rainy, warm day, Krementz was tending the bar when Moore came in a little after one o'clock in the afternoon. The former sergeant ordered a beer and then joined in a card game with a couple of his friends. Not long after Moore entered the bar, Albert Sinex, the seventh and last child of two of New Albany's oldest and most respected citizens, Thomas and Flora Sinex, and a lifelong friend of Moore's, came in the saloon, ordered a beer and stood watching Moore and his card-playing companions.

"I thought you was a church member," Sinex teased his friend.

"I am and thought you was also," Moore replied.

"I am," said Sinex.

The men continued playing and joking with one another for about another fifteen minutes. When Krementz returned from his lunch about one thirty, Moore and Sinex asked the bartender for a pack of cards to play a game called "7 Up"; the loser would pay for the beer. Krementz gave them the cards and then joined them in the game until he had to leave to tend to his bar. Moore and Sinex continued playing, and when Charles Lansford passed through the saloon on his way upstairs to the shop of Charles T. Armstrong, the pair asked him to have a drink with them and join the game. Lansford sat down to play and immediately noticed how quickly the pair drank their beers. He later testified, "Before they got through with that game, they called for beer two or three times. I don't remember which. Moore drank his own beer and mine, too. He would empty his own glass, and seeing mine sitting there, he supposed it was his and drank it."

They continued the game throughout that rainy afternoon. They moved the game to the back room of the saloon, where they continued to talk, laugh and drink more beer. Lansford later claimed the duo drank more than a half a dozen beers while he sat with them, and the already inebriated pair grew drunker with every swallow of the bitter, amber-colored brew. When the conversation turned to politics, a potentially inflammatory subject for the soberest individuals and one definitely best avoided when the participants are drunk, Lansford left the game and moved back into the front room of the saloon.

During the exchange, Moore said he intended to vote for the Democratic candidates for the offices of vice-president and president. Sinex claimed he hadn't decided whom he'd vote for, but he anticipated he'd cast his vote for the Republican candidates, former general Ulysses S. Grant and his running mate, Indiana's Schuyler Colfax, Speaker of the House of the United States House of Representatives. The claim angered the drunken Moore, and he called Sinex a "son of a bitch."

Charles Armstrong, who heard Moore's rude comment as he walked down the stairs from his shop above the bar, didn't pay much attention to the dispute between the two friends. He'd been around drunks long enough to know that their language and play sometimes turned rough. He walked to the front room and began playing the card game "pigeon hole" with three of his friends, among them David Crane and Moore's brother-in-law, Monroe Gwin. As the quartet continued their game, they heard the conversation in the back room growing louder and more heated, and when Moore once more called Sinex a "son of a bitch," Armstrong excused himself from the game and walked to the back room. An obviously intoxicated and angry Moore stood glaring across the table at his drinking companion.

"Thomas, you ought not talk that way," Armstrong told Moore. "Someone might hurt you. Sit down."

Moore refused to sit.

"Oh, no, I would not hurt him. He and I are good friends," Sinex said. "And I will not see him hurt, either."

Moore not only ignored Armstrong's advice but he also looked at Sinex and said, "Not only are you a son of a bitch; you're a Republican son of a bitch!"

Sinex laughed and said, "No, I am not a son of a bitch, but I am a Republican. Now sit down and come and take a glass of beer, and let's be good friends. Come and sit down."

"No. I am not going to sit down," Moore replied.

Sinex stood up and grabbed his friend by the arm, saying in a somewhat less friendly tone than the one he'd used previously, "You have got to sit down."

"Take another drink with me, Thomas," he menacingly demanded of his drunken companion.

"I've had enough," Moore replied. "I'm not going to drink with such a man as you. I want to go."

"Tom, let's take a drink," Sinex said as he came around the table, the card game now over and forgotten.

"No! I want to go. Let go of me. Now!"

Sinex grabbed his buddy's arm, "Come on, you son of a bitch, let's take a drink."

"I don't want a drink. I want to go."

"Well, you can't go until you take one more drink with me."

"Let go of me. You're pulling my shirt out," Moore complained as he struggled against his friend's powerful grasp.

"Don't try to pull away from me, Tom. It's no use. You can't do it," Sinex laughed.

"I don't want to have any difficulty with you," Moore pleaded. "Let me go."

"I don't want any difficulty with you, either. I could whip you in a minute," the muscular Sinex boasted. "But I don't want to."

Moore finally escaped and quickly headed for the front door of the saloon. But his much stronger friend caught him by the neck and forced him into the back room. The pair wrestled for a few minutes. Moore begged Sinex to let him leave, but Albert refused. "Not until you have one more drink with me, Tom," he said as he threw his friend into a chair. Sinex pinned both of Moore's arms and refused to let him go. When he finally loosened his hold, Thomas stood up and drew back his fist as if to strike Albert.

"I'm warning, you, Albert. Let me go!" But his brawny companion grabbed his arm and laughed at the threat from his smaller acquaintance.

Moore, exasperated, agreed to the request, and Sinex ordered more beer. The pair sat down at the table, the scuffle either ignored or forgotten in the pair's drunken haze. Moore then started talking to no one in particular about his experiences at Shiloh.

"That's a goddamned lie, Thomas. You weren't at Shiloh," Sinex teased his friend.

Moore grew angry at his friend's ribbing. "Any person that says I wasn't in that battle is a damned lying son of a bitch."

Sinex continued taunting his friend. "You're lying, Thomas."

"Are you calling me a damned liar?" Moore asked.

Albert drew back his arm as if to strike his companion.

"Don't hit me, Albert."

Putting his arm around Moore, Sinex laughed. "I won't hit you, Thomas. And no one else will either—not as long as I am with you. No one will harm a hair on your head as long as I am with you."

Both men had their arms around each other's waists at this point, and Moore said, "Let me go," but Albert refused to release him. "No. Come and take another drink with me."

Moore looked at Lansford and said, "You are a witness to this. I have asked him to let me go, and he refuses to do it. I don't want to drink with you. I want to leave. Charles and everyone else here is a witness that I asked you to let me go."

Sinex laughed, saying, "Damn the witnesses," then slammed the door leading to the front of the bar. "Moore, you are the craziest man I ever saw when you are drunk!"

"That's no difference to you. Let me go!"

Moore once more escaped from Sinex. He ran toward the closed door, opened it and ran into the front room, but again Sinex caught him and the pair scuffled. Lansford had had enough and went in the front room. Sinex had a tight grip on Moore's head.

"Let him go, Albert," Lansford ordered. "He's had enough."

"I'm not going to let him go until he tucks his shirt back in his pants." Moore's garment had become untucked in the struggle. "I can't let him on the street in this shabby state."

Lansford went in the back room and grabbed Moore's coat. Returning to the front of the saloon, he handed Thomas the coat. "Here, put this on and tuck in your shirt."

"I don't want the damned coat. I just want to leave."

Moore pulled away and ran for the front door, but Sinex again caught him, and another scuffle ensued as Moore tried to remove himself from his friend's tight grasp. Thomas held Albert in a headlock, and Sinex had his arms wrapped around his friend's waist. Their struggle carried them to the door, and the drunken duo stumbled into and through the screen door of the front entrance. They fell to the pavement outside, and the door landed on top of Moore. As he fought to get out from under the door, Sinex got to his feet and approached the struggling young man. He reached down and grabbed Moore by the legs and tried to pull him from under the door. Thomas evaded his friend and kicked at Sinex, who in turn kicked at Moore.

When Krementz lifted the door off him, Moore crawled a short distance before getting to his feet and staggering toward his home across Market Street.

Albert, laughing and dusting himself off, returned inside the saloon. He walked up to the counter and leaned with his left side against the bar. Lansford warned him, "Al, you better go home."

Charles Armstrong echoed the sentiment, "Yes, Al, you had better get out of here."

Albert laughed and said, "Moore isn't coming back. He's an old friend of mine, and I doubt he's coming back."

"Go home, Albert. I'll pay for the beer," Lansford advised his friend. "I'd rather do that than see any more difficulties. How much is the bill, Thomas?" he asked Krementz.

"One dollar and a half," the bartender replied.

Lansford tried to hand Krementz seventy-five cents, but Sinex shoved the money back.

"I'll pay for my own damned beer."

"Albert, I'd much rather pay for the beer than see any more difficulty," Lansford repeated. "Tom went home, and now I want you to go home too."

"You don't suppose he's coming back here, do you?" Sinex asked.

"No, but you know what Tom Moore is when he is drunk," Lansford replied. "You know very well that he is just like a crazy man."

"I'm not afraid of Tom Moore coming back here," Sinex boasted. "He's too big a coward to ever come back to me."

Lansford gave up trying to reason with his drunken friend. He left to close up his carpenter shop behind the saloon.

Charles Armstrong told Krementz, who stood behind Albert, "You had better go out, and if Moore comes back don't let him in." Armstrong then returned to his game, and things apparently settled down.

Lansford closed the side door in the back room. He had just started for the front of the bar when he looked through the front window and saw Moore approaching at a trot from his home across the street. Lansford went out the side door, hoping to head off the determined Moore, but he saw he wouldn't reach the angry drunk in time. He went back in the side door and hollered at Sinex in the front room.

"Albert! Look out! Moore's coming!"

Armstrong happened to look up from his game in time to see Moore standing in the doorway, pistol in hand. "Look out, Al! Here he comes with a pistol!"

The customers in the saloon all tried to make their way out of the bar—all except Albert, who calmly stood at the counter and looked at Thomas. "Come and have a drink with me," Sinex said to his drunken childhood friend.

Moore raised his pistol, a Colt revolver with a six-inch barrel, and pointed it at Sinex. Armstrong tried to grab for the weapon, but Moore fired the weapon before he could reach the gun. Armstrong took hold of the barrel of the revolver with his left hand and wrapped his right around the gun's cylinder. Throwing the intoxicated assailant to the ground, he held him down and turned to Sinex. "Al, you are shot!"

Sinex said nothing. He slowly walked toward the pair, and before Armstrong could get the pistol from the shooter's hand, Sinex jumped on Armstrong and started biting his cheek. Armstrong called for Krementz to come and help him take the weapon away from Moore as he continued to struggle with Sinex. Charles's brother Thomas then rushed to his sibling's aid.

"Let go, Al. Don't bite Charlie," Armstrong's brother said as he attempted to grab the gun. Charles told him, "Never mind, I've got it."

Krementz and Thomas Armstrong finally pulled Albert off Charles. The wounded drunk walked slowly back toward the counter. Charles Armstrong turned to Lansford, saying, "Here, take this revolver," and then walked over to Sinex and asked, "Are you really shot?"

Albert answered, "I am shot pretty bad."

The bullet had struck Sinex between the sixth and seventh ribs on his right side, passed through his lungs and liver and lodged in his spine near the seventh rib. Though extremely painful, the wound didn't prove immediately fatal. Monroe Gwin and Thomas Armstrong caught hold of Albert on either side and walked him outside. Albert shook his assistants off and walked up the street about seven paces, then started to collapse. Gwin rushed to his aid and prevented him from falling to the pavement. Thomas Armstrong ran up and helped Gwin support the stout Sinex as the trio walked to Dr. Meurer's office.

"Where is the doctor? This man has been shot."

Told that Dr. Meurer wasn't in his office, they returned to the Belvidere, and as they got to the saloon's second door, Albert's legs folded under him and he fell to the pavement, crying out as he did so, "I'm gone! I'm gone!"

Gwin and Armstrong poured water on his head and then picked him up and carried him across the street to Gwin's stables, where they laid him on a bench in the office. John Rodgers came in and tried to talk to Sinex. Rodgers knew Albert would soon die and wanted to talk to him about death, but Sinex made no reply. When someone told Rodgers that Sinex was drunk, he abandoned the attempt to help Albert make peace with his God.

Hearing the commotion, James Spencer entered the office and saw Sinex lying on the wooden bench. "Who done that to you, Al?" he asked, as James Meekin walked in the office.

"Thomas Moore has killed me," the mortally wounded man replied. "Oh my God, Tom. What could you have done this for?"

Charles Lansford entered the office about this time and gave the weapon to William Merker, who had come in earlier.

"That's Moore's pistol," Thomas Armstrong told him, "Don't let anyone have it."

Merker sat the pistol on the desk in the office, and the men stood around watching their friend slowly and painfully die.

After shooting his friend, Moore stood outside the door for only a moment or two before walking back into the bar.

"Where is my coat?" he asked the stunned Krementz.

"It's in the back room lying on a chair. Thomas, I believe you have killed Albert."

Moore made no reply. He retrieved his coat and then walked out the front door. His wife called to him from their home across the street, and the young assailant walked slowly to his house, never looking back. As he crossed the street, his father-in-law walked toward the saloon. Moore either didn't see him or ignored him on purpose.

"What's the matter, Thomas?" Gwin asked.

"He was beating the shit out of me and I wasn't going to stand it."

"How'd you get in this fuss?"

"They were beating me. I fixed him."

"Yes, Tom, you have fixed yourself. That's what you have done."

"I am not going to be abused or imposed upon."

"You have done it," and with that, the conversation between the two ended. Moore went into his house but returned a couple minutes later followed by his wife, Elizabeth. History leaves us no record of the words that passed between them, but he must have told her he'd shot his friend. Witnesses claimed Elizabeth stopped and then fell to the ground. Her husband headed down the alley between East Second and East Third Streets toward Main Street.

Thomas Moore headed east on Main Street for about a block and then entered Alexander's Drugstore near the northeast corner of East Fourth and Main Streets. He walked up to the third floor, moved some bottles and demijohns (large bottles, usually with a capacity of between five and fifteen gallons and commonly used to brew beer or make wine) from the south side of the room, lay down behind them with his head pointed to the west and passed out.

He lay there in his drunken stupor until awakened by New Albany Police officer Stewart Sandford. Informed of the shooting by a small boy, the policeman, after questioning several witnesses, found Moore in his hiding place.

"Tom, what are you doing here?" the officer asked.

"I am drunk."

"You are not so very drunk, Tom."

Moore began to rise, and Sandford, suspicious of his intent, asked, "Have you got a pistol?"

"No, I haven't," Moore answered as he unsteadily rose to his feet.

"How in the name of God, Tom, came you to shoot Al Sinex?"

"I shot him in self-defense."

"Has there ever been any former difficulty between you two?"

Moore hung his head and said softly, "No."

As they walked down the stairs, Sandford noticed several cuts and scratches on one side of Moore's face and neck. The wounds appeared to have been inflicted with fingernails.

"How did you come by those, Tom?"

"Al did it. He had me down and grabbed me by the neck and scratched me."

Sandford took his prisoner to the jail, where Sheriff Thomas J. Fullenlove;[4] Colonel DeWitt C. Anthony, a former lieutenant colonel of the Twenty-third Indiana Infantry regiment and also a veteran of Shiloh; and William H. Hale, who served with Moore in the Twenty-third, interrogated the prisoner. All three men later testified that Moore seemed intoxicated, but Hale claimed he couldn't tell if the prisoner was too drunk to know right from wrong. "He answered the questions I propounded him intelligently." However, Colonel Anthony stated, "I talked with him and tried to get a statement of the difficulty but could get no intelligent account of him. I could only get a statement that he had been choked and beat, but he seemed to have no intelligent knowledge of the difficulty."

While Moore underwent the interrogation at the jail, Albert Sinex lay dying in the offices of Berry Gwin's stables. No one mentioned to Sinex that he wouldn't live through the night, but even in his drunken condition, he knew. He asked his friends to take him to the home on the corner of East Sixth and Water Streets that he shared with his wife, the former Christa E. McArthur, and his daughter, Mittie Ford.[5] About six o'clock that evening, his friends loaded him into the back of a wagon, and I can only imagine the excruciating pain young Albert endured as he lay atop the rough boards, the bullet lodged in his spine, as the conveyance bounced along the bumpy, unpaved roadway. Though the journey must have been agonizing for him, he lived long enough to make it to his once happy home, where, at a little after seven o'clock that night, he finally, mercifully, breathed his last breath as his grieving family and friends sat by his side.

His funeral was held two days later at Centenary Methodist Church, which his family had attended since the building's construction in 1837.

A large number of New Albanians attended the service, conducted by the Reverend J.H. Clippinger in the absence of the church's regular pastor, Reverend James Hill. The *New Albany Daily Ledger* said of the service:

> *All in attendance seemed duly impressed with the solemnity of the occasion. The anguish of his young wife, and venerable parents, and brothers and sisters, who were thus so suddenly and terribly bereft, brought tears to the eyes of most of those in attendance. We trust it may never be our lot to witness another such soul harrowing scene.*

What the paper did not mention is where his family buried the twenty-seven-year-old Albert Sinex. It's logical to assume his family buried him in the Sinex family's huge vault at the Fairview Cemetery, but the cemetery records do not reflect that fact. Neither does any other documentation I have uncovered reveal where Sinex's remains might lie. But just because I can find no evidence that proves one way or the other where his body rests doesn't mean he isn't entombed there. The cemetery's record keeping during this time period was haphazard, to say the least, and I find it hard to believe that the family would have constructed the costly vault where they intended the remains of the clan members should spend their eternal slumbers and not put their youngest child within its brick walls.

The editor of the *New Albany Daily Ledger* offered a glimpse into the defense strategy when, writing in his paper just two days after the murder on Wednesday, July 29, he claimed:

> *No other reason or excuse than the crazed condition of Moore from frequent potations of liquor, can be urged for the commission of the crime. Indeed, yesterday morning Moore said repeatedly and earnestly, and, as we believe, sincerely, that he had no recollection of the unfortunate and fatal affair. In speaking to us of it he said: "This was all caused by whiskey."*
> *And what a sermon is there in those few words! Here were two young men, both of the most amiable dispositions when sober, both members of the same church, both suddenly overtaken by the same temptation, and led on in that temptation by the same mysterious, insane, insatiable demon of desire that knows no abatement but satiety; forgetting vows, and God, and heaven, and together drowning the stings of conscious in the cup that poisons the*

*soul and fits the mind for deeds that in the man's sober moments he would shrink form in horror. This was the status of these two young men on the fatal afternoon of Monday. Who is safe that puts the poisoned chalice to his lips and quaffs its soul-killing contents? Had it not been for liquor two heretofore happy families would not to-day be bowed under the deepest grief, and two young men, both calculated for useful members of society, would not be virtually dead—for young Sinex in his winding sheet is no more dead to society than young Moore, in his narrow prison cell.*

The preliminary examination of Thomas P. Moore, for shooting and killing Albert L. Sinex, began on Thursday, August 6, 1868, a little less than two weeks after the crime, in the police courtroom, with the Honorable A.W. Monroe, justice of the peace, presiding. A large throng of people crowded the small courtroom.

The defense team, composed of John S. Davis and Colonel Anthony, entered a plea of not guilty on their client's behalf. They didn't deny Moore shot Sinex but instead relied on Indiana law, which at the time claimed anyone under the influence of alcohol was not in his right mind and could indeed be considered temporarily insane; therefore, he was not accountable for his actions while under the influence of the drug. Most of the witnesses they brought forth testified that the twenty-five year-old father of one was drunk out of his mind at the time of the shooting.

The prosecution for the state, led by Colonel Thomas J. Jackson, prosecutor for the common pleas court, denied that Moore was drunk out of his mind and produced several witnesses who disputed the defense team's assertion. The prosecution must have felt it had won when, the following Monday, August 11, Justice of the Peace Monroe denied bail to Moore. Justice Monroe stated:

*The court has been very careful in the examination of the law in this case, especially the practice of our own worthy Judge, Judge Bicknell. He says, on page 287, many of the cases in which the unlawful killing is murder have been referred to in stating the distinctions in reference to manslaughter and justifiable and excusable homicide (which we have carefully examined.) He says so far as the general character of the act is concerned, that whenever a human being is killed by an act accompanied with an unlawful intention to kill, such a homicide is murder. The Court is of the opinion that such was the case with the defendant according to the evidence, and therefore we find the defendant, Thomas P. Moore, guilty of murder in the first degree.*

Moore's defense team claimed the decision in direct opposition to the evidence presented and the state law. It sued for a writ of habeas corpus and requested that Judge George Augustus Bicknell hear the case upon his return to the city from his tour of the circuit.

Not long after his return, Judge Bicknell granted Moore's bail, and a little over a year later, he agreed with the defense's claim that Moore was drunk out of his mind and therefore not responsible for his actions. Bicknell absolved Thomas Moore of any guilt or legal responsibility for the shooting death of Albert Sinex.

Thomas P. Moore stayed in New Albany. Ironically, in light of what had happened, in the spring of 1875, Thomas Moore, along with his partner, Charles Sohn, applied for and received a license to sell liquor in New Albany. They opened a bar on the northwest corner of Bank and Market Streets. Thomas and Elizabeth had four more children in the ensuing years—two daughters, Anna and Francis,[6] and two more sons, Marshall and Frank. Anna died of a brain aneurism in early February 1887, but their four remaining children stood by his bedside when Thomas died of tuberculosis in his home at 409 East Fourth Street on the afternoon of Saturday, July 8, 1916. His family held his funeral in the same church where his victim's service was held, Centenary Methodist, and he was buried at the Fairview Cemetery next to Elizabeth, who had preceded him in death on Sunday, January 30, of that same year after a long, unspecified illness.

## The "Happy Home Converted into a Hell by the Demon Whisky."

Jacob Ritter made his way from his German homeland to New Albany sometime in the middle of the nineteenth century. On April 30, 1861, a little more than two weeks after the commencement of hostilities in the American Civil War, he married Catherine Mensinger, daughter of a respected middle-class New Albany family. Ritter, described as an "industrious stonecutter," worked hard at his craft, and his steady labor soon enabled the couple to purchase a small home where "peace and prosperity reigned" for a number of years.

After a long day at work, like many working-class men and women, Jacob enjoyed an adult beverage (or two, or more) after his supper. Pleasantly buzzed and satisfied with his life, Jacob and his wife spent most nights enjoying a quiet and uneventful evening. At least, they did for the first few years of their marriage. Then Jacob's drinking grew out of control, and according to a byline in the *New Albany Daily Ledger Standard*, the Ritters' "Happy Home Converted into a Hell by the Demon Whisky."

Jacob neglected his business and his wife. He spent more and more of his time in the local saloons instead of at home with Catherine and quickly gained a reputation as a loafer and a drunkard. Pleasant evenings once spent in the company of his loving spouse turned into nights of debauchery in the company of thieves, scoundrels and other less desirable elements of New Albany society. Jacob spent many nights lodged in the Floyd County Jail on charges of drunkenness and/or cruelty toward Catherine. The once happy marriage became a living hell for her. She endured a tortured existence at the hands of the man she'd once loved with all her heart, until finally, in 1873, unable to tolerate any longer the nightmare that her marriage had become, she filed for divorce.

Catherine remained in the home she had shared with Jacob while he slept wherever he passed out. The "humble, yet honorable manner, in which she was trying to obtain a livelihood, rendered her an object of pity in the eyes of all well-disposed people," and her neighbors helped her when and how they could. Many of the city's merchants, aware of her "unapproachable character" and the unfortunate turn her life had taken because of her husband's uncontrollable drinking, furnished her with enough work sewing that she was able to maintain a meager, though comfortable, existence.

Despite the divorce, Jacob continued to abuse his former wife. Drunk out of his mind, he'd return on occasion to his once happy abode to mistreat Catherine in "a manner too terrible to describe. The scenes enacted would make angels weep, and the very hosts of hell rejoice. His soul seemed possessed by a thousand devils, and every demon was busily at work in changing a happy home from a paradise to a hell." Jacob "seemed to take delight in this nefarious work, and it seemed as though he wanted to drive to destruction the being who has used all honorable means to rid herself of his fiendish grasp." Catherine, still in love with Jacob despite his cruelty, tried desperately to calm her out-of-control former spouse, and when she'd withstood all of the abuse humanly possible, she'd finally call the police and cry as she watched the officers carry him off to jail.

Jacob Ritter, continuing his descent into madness, became convinced that his wife was a witch. In a later interview with Father Doebbner of St. Mary's Catholic Church, Ritter stated, "I have been for one year troubled with witches, and during that time they drove me from one place to another, and they wouldn't let me work." Believing several other New Albanians were also witches, he left the city for Cincinnati, Ohio, where he stayed for several months, continuing his heavy drinking. Despite the distance between them, Ritter claimed Catherine "did trouble me the whole of nights with her witchcraft."

He wrote several letters in his native German to many of New Albany's residents, including Catherine. Most of the missives, upon interpretation, proved nothing more than the incoherent ramblings of a mind gone insane. In one, he claimed Catherine and her brother, Gotleib Mensinger, wrongfully blamed him for the couple's troubles. In another, Ritter claimed his former wife cursed him, stating, "As long as I lived I must have witches or become a witch. I didn't want that." In a rather lucid message addressed to New Albany mayor William B. Richardson, Ritter informed the mayor that he, Ritter, intended to return to the city. Ritter requested that Richardson keep the town's "little witches and devils" from bothering him upon his return. No record of the mayor's reaction remains, but I assume he notified the police department of the lunatic's impending return before tossing the letter aside.

Ritter walked from Cincinnati to Louisville, Kentucky, and finally arrived in New Albany sometime during the evening of Wednesday, September 22, 1875. He went to Catherine's home and begged her to let him stay. She relented to his repeated entreaties and let him stay. They talked about their situation, and he told her she had "bewitched and bothered him for a long time." When he asked her to "let me go," she made no response to his request for several moments and then told him, "I can do nothing for you." At some point that Friday, he either left of his own accord or she convinced him to go.

When he returned about midnight "crazed with rum," Catherine refused her husband entry into the house, but Ritter, "a powerful man," despite his intemperate habits of the last few years, forced his way in. Jacob "first commenced his fiendish work by beating the unfortunate woman in a manner most terrible." The drunken madman continued to beat her for the next several hours, and though the neighbors in the heavily populated neighborhood of moderate houses built close together heard her screams, none of them came to her assistance or called the police. Strangely, Catherine didn't call the police or ask any of her neighbors for help.

Neighbor Oliver Cassell's wife heard Jacob speaking in German about 5:00 a.m., and though she didn't speak the language, she thought he sounded angry. Oliver heard the couple talking about 5:30 a.m., and I can only assume that shortly after the Cassells heard the couple, Catherine either passed out or Jacob allowed her to go to bed. What I do know is that when he heard the steady breathing that indicated she was sleeping, he wrapped a strip of bleached muslin around her neck and strangled her.

However, he didn't quite complete the job.

Though he'd thought her dead after his strenuous exertions, something convinced him that she still lived. Perhaps she gasped as she struggled to get air through her crushed windpipe. Maybe she moaned in agony. Whatever she did convinced him that she still lived. Jacob "then took some heavy instrument, probably an axe or a hatchet, and beat her head into a perfect jelly." Catherine's skull had five large holes, and her face "was mutilated in a most horrible manner." This time, his efforts paid off; when he finished the brutal assault, Catherine Ritter was finally, mercifully, dead.

Satisfied he'd finally killed her, Jacob sat down and wrote the following in a "large, coarse, German, sprawling hand." Adam Werner, editor of the *Deutsch Zeitung*, translated the letter:

> *I have killed my wife because she is a witch. She persecuted me for eleven months. I have burned her up because burning shall be the reward of all witches, which was the rule when the human race was wiser. At present we claim that we have so advanced and are still so ignorant as not to believe in witches any more. Gotleib Mensinger is a witch also; he was with the whole compoodle. There is a good many more witches in New Albany yet. The half of the city is full of them. My wife cheated me, and her brother was the whole cause of it. Don't want any of my wife's bones laid by the side of mine, for she is the biggest witch in New Albany, and her brother,*

*Gotleib Mensinger, is also a great witch. Witches would even follow me to St. Louis and wherever I go. When I traveled from St. Louis to Cincinnati and Covington and from there to Louisville on foot, my intention of coming back to New Albany. Jake Herter is a witch also. I will close my letter with the hope that God Almighty will forgive me, for I have never wronged anybody yet. I ask all honorable and Christian people for forgiveness. This is the whole truth and the way the witches have persecuted me. This is all true—as true as there is a God in heaven. John Rippberger and others are witches. I, Jacob Reitter, testify in the name of the Trinity Gods herewith, that I will not speak else but the truth, so help me God. These are the names of the witches: Catherine Reitter, born Mensinger and two of her brothers, Gotleib Mensinger and frow [sic] and Catherine Mensinger, a widow woman and Taylor Belzar, wife and daughter. The daughter is married to a carpenter by the name of Rickey. Belzar's father-in-law, old man Bergley and wife and four great grand children, Bunkle wife and son, Shoemaker, born Trinler and son, a man named Sass and son, Theobold, stonemason, shoemaker Esbach, John Rippberger and wife, Theobold, frow [sic] and son. The man that finds this give it to the officers of the court.*

Jacob placed the letter in an envelope, along with his fire insurance papers, and wrote on the back of the envelope, "German Mutual Fire Insurance Company, of Indiana; Policy No. 1414, to Katherine Ritter, $550; commences Aug. 28, 1878. John Horn, agent." On the front, Jacob directed that the contents be returned to the proper authorities.

Tucking the envelope in his pocket, he turned his attention to his wife's still warm corpse, lying on the bed where the pair once shared their most intimate moments. He carefully arranged her body, and a little before six o'clock that morning, he set fire to the house in an attempt to cover his crime. Though he had just brutally murdered his ex-wife, on his way out the back door, he stopped to grab the cage containing her pet canary.

Her neighbors finally called the police, but only after the first of them smelled smoke.

Neighbor Nick Clouse had been awake about fifteen minutes when he smelled smoke. Quickly putting on his clothes, he ran to the Ritter house and beat on the door. Receiving no answer, he broke down the door and saw Catherine lying dead on her bed. By this time, two other neighbors had arrived, including Henry Walter, and the three men carried Catherine's lifeless form out of the smoke-filled house. According to the account in the *New Albany Daily Ledger Standard*, "her flesh was burnt to a crisp in many places, and she presented a scene that beggars description. She was placed on a bed in the street and covered with a rough blanket, and hundreds of spectators stopped to behold the scene, and then turned away heartsick."

Jacob watched all the commotion from his hiding spot in the chicken yard along the right side of the property in the backyard. He'd placed the cage holding the canary next to a fencepost, along with a pocketbook holding several letters, and then secreted himself in the chicken yard. We can't be sure how long he lay there, but at some point during all of the commotion, guilt overcame Jacob Ritter, and he pulled his old Barlow pocketknife out and slit his throat!

The cold steel sliced deeply through the soft flesh of his neck just below his larynx, the deep gash partially severing his windpipe. According to a physician who later examined him, Jacob suffered the following injury:

> *The left ala of the thyroid-hyoid cartilage was fractured longitudinally one-third of the way from the median projection, completely shutting off the rimatid glottis. The platysmo myoides, the sterno cleiodo-mastoid, the anterior belly of the omo-hyoid, the stern-hyoid, and the sterno-thyroid muscle were completely severed. The trapezius muscle was not examined.*

This is normally where one expects the story to end, for anyone suffering such a horrendous wound, even with today's modern medical techniques, usually dies from such a catastrophic injury. However, the Fates hadn't finished with Jacob Ritter.

Police officer Peter Weber assumed Ritter dead when he found the murderer lying on his right side in a rapidly expanding pool of blood in the filthy chicken yard. Imagine the officer's surprise when he rolled Ritter over on his back and the supposedly dead man spoke! Weber looked at Jacob and said, "This is a nice fix you're in." Jacob tried to speak, but the officer couldn't understand the killer's garbled whisper, so Ritter motioned toward the fence. Weber walked over to the spot indicated, found the package of letters and called for assistance. A crowd gathered in response to Weber's call, but Ritter, his throat slashed open, blood pouring down his chest from the wound, "glared at them like a gladiator" and motioned them away. He was bound and taken to the county jail.

The authorities summoned Drs. Easley and Lemon to the jail. The pair found Ritter "struggling for breath and floundering around in his own blood." The physicians sewed shut the gaping wound but determined that death would likely occur within the next few hours. Following their Hippocratic oath, they did what they could to make their patient comfortable before leaving him so they could attend a hastily summoned coroner's inquest into the death of Catherine Ritter.

Coroner Pennington called the jurors—John Saunders, Adam Lambert, John Hoffman, Tobias Schmadel, Frederick Newhouse and B.J. Sheppard—along with several witnesses, including officer Weber, the Cassells, Nick Clouse, Mrs. Catherine Belvis and both doctors, to his inquest in order to determine what happened in the hours leading up to Catherine's death, as well as the cause of death. Dr. Easley expressed his opinion that Catherine Ritter had died of strangulation but hastened to add that he'd only had time to make a cursory examination.

The doctors returned to the jail expecting their patient to have expired, but to their surprise, they found him resting comfortably—at least, as comfortable as possible for a man with such a severe wound. Though he could speak in an almost inaudible whisper and had taken several small swallows of water, both doctors assured those in attendance that their patient had no chance for a recovery and would likely not survive the morning. Everyone appeared certain that before lunch, "the wretch will appear before a just God to atone for his terrible crime."

Dr. Easley left the jail to perform a more thorough inspection of the body of Catherine Ritter. After the examination, Easley concluded that her killer had strangled her almost to the point of death while she slept and then killed her by striking her repeatedly about the head with an unknown blunt object.

Despite the pair of physicians' predictions that he would expire before nightfall, Jacob Ritter surprised everyone by living through what must have been an agonizing day for him. Two days after Catherine's murder and Jacob's attempted suicide, the *New Albany Daily Ledger Standard* reported:

> *During the day Reitter* [sic] *has at times showed symptoms of recovery, and at other times he has suffered the most intense pain. A* LEDGER-STANDARD

*reporter called at the jail just before going to press, and the miserable man was in a sitting posture, trying to swallow some nourishment. His breathing is heavy and his pulse irregular. If the distorted features of all the fiends of the infernal regions could be combined, they could not possibly present a scene more terrible. His face and neck is very much swollen, and his skin has become very dark. As he rolls his large white eyes, half in pain and half in horror, it naturally causes a person to shrink from his presence as from the evil one. He does not seem to fully realize his terrible condition, or if he does, he cares but little about it. The physicians say he may survive through the night, or possibly two or three days, but death is certain in a very short time. May God have mercy on the soul of the blood-stained wretch.*

New Albanians watching the case read with amazement the next day when the paper reported Ritter's condition much improved. According to the article, Ritter ate two meals and walked around the jail, and "there don't seem to be much the matter with him at first sight, but when he throws his head back, you can see that his neck is half cut off."

However, the information proved wrong. The following day, the paper printed a correction:

*We are informed that our report of the condition of Reitter [sic] published yesterday, is calculated to create the impression that he would recover. He did not, as stated, take in two square meals and walk around the hall of the jail. Likewise we were in error in stating that the probabilities were that he would not be planted. On the contrary, his condition has been from the first, such as to preclude any hope of recovery.*

He continued suffering for the next several weeks, fading away slowly in his cell. New Albany's eager citizens pored over the daily paper for accounts of the prisoner. Six days after the murder, they read the following account of Ritter's existence:

*If there is a miserable wretch between earth and eternity, his name is Jacob Reitter [sic], who has been languishing in the county jail for the past week. The triple crime of murder, arson, and suicide rests upon his guilty soul. He neither lives nor can he die, but is suffering all the agonies of death and hell combined. Our reporter called at the jail this afternoon and found him sitting in a chair, nursing his head over a bucket of water, looking the picture of despair and wretchedness. He cannot talk, but his look indicates that at last he has come to a full sense of his awful crime, and if there is any such thing as preparation for such a sinner to visit the world beyond our vision, he is studying the matter most intently and prayerfully. He is tired of this world of sin and sorrow, and desires to be delivered of its cares and torments as he realizes them at present.*

*Yesterday he begged for a knife to complete the job he undertook a few days ago, and intimated that if he could secure a weapon he would make sure work of his earthly existence in quick time. Though hardly ready, he is willing to take the chances of the dread hereafter...How a man with his head partly severed from his body can live is more than the doctors can solve, and the general opinion is that he may die at any moment, and yet he may exist for days.*

Ritter asked for a Lutheran minister, but none answered his summons. That night, Dr. Easley again sewed up the wound in the prisoner's throat and placed a tube in his windpipe; "the flesh about his throat and windpipe is very much mortified, and in places is perfectly rotten and will not hold a thread."

The next day, Father Doebbener, of the Spring Street Catholic Church, who'd read of Ritter's unanswered request for a minister, visited Ritter and told him he'd to anything for him within his power. The priest later defended the action in a note to the papers:

*Christ the Lord says I am come not to save the righteous but to seek after those that are lost. The healthy need no physician, but the sick have need of one. This authority gave he then to his established church, to save sinners even the greatest. Why then should a priest of this church not look after the condition of men.*

Moved by Father Doebbener's speech, Ritter burst into tears. The priest then asked Ritter if he was a Catholic by birth, and the prisoner "looked strangely at his questioner, rolled his large eyes and shook his head. When asked if anything could be done for him, and if the services of a priest were desired he again acted as before and shook his head."

Father Doebbener then handed Ritter a pencil and paper, and the killer wrote:

> *I have been for one year troubled with witches, and during that time they drove me from one place to another, and they wouldn't let me work. Then I went to Springfield, Ohio, but my wife did trouble me the whole of nights with her witchcraft. The next morning she blamed me, she and her brother, and said as long as I lived I must have witches or to become a witch. I didn't want that. Then she told me that we had only separated by table and bed, but the value of my little house should go to the children of her sister. Then I went back to New Albany, and was with her for three days. I often told her that she had bewitched me and bothered me for a long time. Then I tell you and assure you before Almighty that no man in the United States has had such trouble as I have. When I told her to let me go, she said nothing. When I came she said I can do nothing for you. In the morning she wanted to drive me away but I felt like I could not go. Then she wanted to call a watchman. And Father I don't know how things went after that, but I feel no sin, except as any one commits a sin. But as long as I have lived I have not betrayed any man—didn't steal anything or kill anyone. I have lived here for fifteen years and have offended no one.*

After Father Doebbener left the jail, Ritter became sullen and whispered to another prisoner, a man known only as Miller, that he didn't want any priest or preacher. He wanted to die and claimed if he could get a knife he would cut his throat or hang himself if he could get a rope. Ritter said he'd tired of this world and was willing to risk the consequences of the life hereafter. Miller probably would have gladly helped Ritter die if he could, for, as a reporter informed his reading public, Ritter "is a horrible sight to look upon, and is very offensive to those who go near his rotting carcass."

Jacob Ritter finally died on November 23, 1875, almost two months after killing his wife and attempting to end his own by slicing his throat in a manner most painful. The *New Albany Daily Ledger Standard* reported his passing with the following comments:

> *The lights are out, the curtain has fallen; the last actor of the terrible tragedy enacted a few weeks ago has crossed the boundaries of the wonderful*

*beyond. Jacob Reitter, the wife murderer, the incendiary and suicide, is dead. The pale, sickening light, as it found its way into the hall of the jail this morning, disclosed the sallow features of the dead murderer, as he lay stretched upon a rude pallet surrounded by a crowd of curiosity-seeking spectators. His head was thrown back, which plainly revealed the terrible wound across his throat, which had been self-inflicted, and which caused his death. The same grim, stolid look of determination, that was noticeable on his features in life, marked them in death. Long hours of pain and anguish had reduced the powerful man to a mere skeleton—haggard in its appearance and bearing the outward marks of long suffering and sin. His Herculean strength was all that prolonged his life, which only made the punishment for his bloody crime more severe. We know but little of his mental or physical sufferings, and can only judge by the deep, dark traces that they have left. The wound in his throat never became entirely healed, and from the first his physician said it was only a matter of time in regard to his taking off. He had a bad cough, and at times was unable to expectorate. His voice was gone, and the last act of his life, while sitting in a chair, at half-past 9 o'clock this morning, was to write the following, in German, which being translated, reads: "Give me some more of those brown powders, so that I can get relief in breathing." He had hardly finished writing the words, when he dropped from the chair and died without a struggle. We understand that a post mortem examination will be held this evening, which will probably demonstrate the fact that he died from suffocation, occasioned by the wound in his throat. Thus has passed away one of the most terrible actors that has ever figured in the annals of crime. The details setting forth the horrors of that crime have been read and reread, and to-day the miserable wretch has been called hence to account for his crimes in the presence of a just God. Neither time nor eternity will obscure his sin, and it is useless to give an account of it now. All that was mortal of the murderer has passed from earth, and we have no right to judge of the soul. All bitter feeling should now be banished from our breasts, all utterances of censure should now be hushed, for the guilty being who sinned, struggled and suffered is no more. The jury summoned to investigate the causes which lead to Reiter's death, after having heard the evidence and examined the body, decided that said deceased came to his death from fatty degeneration of the heart, superinduced by wounds inflicted upon himself.*

Jacob Ritter received no formal funeral, and the paper makes no mention of anyone mourning his passing. Though a monument may once have marked his final resting place in the pauper's section of the Fairview Cemetery in New Albany, nothing remains today to note where the killer now sleeps his eternal slumber.

# It Was a Dark and Stormy Night—Really!

It hadn't started out that way when Nathaniel T. Johnson and his brother James settled themselves among the tombstones near one of the three iron-gated entryways on the Eighth Street side of the city's Northern Burial Grounds, where rests the mortal remains of many of New Albany's most important and influential citizens, as well as those who in various ways were not quite the town's best representatives. The men entered the cemetery about eight o'clock that Saturday evening in order to keep a sharp lookout on the grave of their brother, thirty-year-old Thomas Johnson, who'd died unexpectedly the previous week in Chicago, Illinois, leaving behind a distraught widow and one child. William Deeble, an employee of the cemetery, joined the brothers, the trio hiding in the darkened shadows near the entrance.

About two hundred yards farther into the silent grounds, city police officers Michael Hennessey and Thomas Cannon, accompanied by Elmer Hopper, kept close watch on the grave of former New Albany police officer thirty-two-year-old Edwin Pierce, who'd died, as expected, of consumption about eight o'clock in the morning of the day before, Friday, February 21, 1891. Pierce's funeral had just been held during the sunny afternoon preceding that dark and stormy Saturday night.

Typical of the rapidly changing spring weather in the Ohio River Valley, the clear skies the residents of the city had enjoyed earlier that evening clouded over, and shortly after the nervously waiting men heard the bells of nearby St. Mary's Church toll eleven o'clock, a violent tempest—described by the *New Albany Tribune* the next day as "a storm of more than ordinary severity"—ripped through the area. Jagged forks of lightning, followed by deafening thunder claps, ripped apart the inky black stillness in the graveyard, and a rain the city's papers labeled as "torrential downpours" forced the two separate groups to seek shelter under tarpaulins the group of watchmen had brought with them. Despite the tempest, all six remained determined to steadfastly maintain their vigils in the burial ground throughout the night. No matter how terrible the storm or how miserable the conditions, these men considered their work a matter of personal honor and duty to a recently departed friend and/or brother.

Men in the Victorian era were often more emotionally attached to their close male friends than are today's men and were more likely to express those feelings. Their diaries and the letters they exchanged often contain expressions of love and friendship that many today consider evidence of homosexuality. While this may indeed be the case in some situations, it most definitely is not the case in others. Based on the emotion and devotion expressed in several letters to his close friend Joshua Speed, some recent historians have used those writings to portray Abraham Lincoln as a homosexual, though there is no other evidence to suggest either man was gay. Such emotional attachments often motivated men in the Gilded Age to sometimes drastic actions in defense of such a close friend, and deterring these vigilant guardians from standing watch over the recently interred remains of their loved ones that dark and stormy night would have required much more than a rainstorm, for these watchmen had been alerted that ghouls intent on a ghastly booty lurked in the flickering shadows of New Albany's gas-lit streets that sinister and wild night. The steadfast sentinels swore they'd catch the grave robbers, who earlier that day had expressed an interest in snatching from their resting places the buried corpses of their former comrades and kin.

Not long after noon that sunny Saturday a well-dressed gentleman appeared at the office door of Colonel Dan Shrader, the cemetery's sexton (or caretaker), and inquired where he might find Deeble. Shrader told the inquisitive visitor that Deeble could likely be found somewhere in the northern part of the grounds, then watched with amusement as the young dandy confidently strode off in the direction indicated. The sexton watched the nattily attired young man stroll away and later claimed that he'd thought it somewhat odd when the fancy little man had stopped only a short distance away to study rather intensely the area surrounding the freshly turned dirt atop Pierce's new grave, but being a busy man with much to do, Shrader turned his attentions back to the business of tending to the final resting places of the city's dearly departed.

The dapper young fellow, later identified as Dr. J.T. Blackburn of nearby Louisville, Kentucky, found his quarry on the cemetery's main avenue and asked Deeble if he would direct him to the graves of Pierce and Johnson. Deeble, believing Blackburn a friend of the deceased, agreed to show the visitor to the graves and later swore under oath that he'd been surprised when, arriving at Pierce's grave, Blackburn had offered him two dollars, which Deeble claimed the physician peeled off a rather large and impressive roll of bills. Deeble claimed he had initially refused the money, telling the doctor he was simply doing his duty, but Blackburn insisted that Deeble accept the money in payment "for the trouble of walking two hundred yards with me." The hard-toiling cemetery worker finally accepted the doctor's money as the physician continued talking.

Blackburn told Deeble that the conscientious worker could make a large amount of money in the coming months if he could remain absolutely silent about what he was about to hear. According to Deeble, Blackburn explained that the medical schools in Louisville had "played out" the Walnut Ridge Cemetery in Jeffersonville, Indiana, and Dr. Blackburn and his colleagues were now so desperate for bodies for the dissecting labs at the colleges that they would gladly pay Deeble twenty dollars apiece for the corpses of Pierce and Johnson. The best part was that Deeble wouldn't have to do anything but keep watch while the ghouls went about their ghastly task—that and keep quiet about the whole affair. If he could do that, there would be more such assignments in the future, and the low-paid laborer could make quite a tidy little sum with little effort. If Deeble cooperated, not only would he make some much-needed money, but also there was no way anyone would know what had transpired because these body-snatchers were as practiced and talented in their black arts as in their trained profession. They were so good, in fact, that generally no one ever knew when a cemetery had been robbed.

The thieves first carefully removed the flowers adorning the freshly turned earth before removing any sod covering, setting the blooms and sections of grass aside as they rapidly went about their ghastly work. As quiet as the corpse they sought, the desperados swiftly removed the dirt covering the coffin and then silently broke open the casket. The fiends quickly removed the corpse, closed the lid on the now empty box and then hastily and quietly filled in the gaping black hole. They returned the sod to its former place atop the now empty grave and placed the flowers back atop the dirt, with none but the ghouls aware of the desecration. To this day, no one can say with any certainty whether or not a body lies beneath every tombstone in the Fairview Cemetery. No one knows for sure if the corpses once buried there, meant to rest in peace in their graves for eternity, still lie beneath the ground or ended up resting in pieces in one of the dissection laboratories in the Louisville medical schools.

Deeble quickly agreed to Blackburn's request, though he later claimed he did so only in order to garner enough information to successfully trap and prosecute Blackburn and his gang. Blackburn, apparently satisfied with Deeble's feigned willingness, walked the short distance to the gate on Eighth Street, jumped the fence and then turned back to study the position of the graves one more time before moving off in a southerly direction.

Deeble immediately set off in search of Shrader. He informed the caretaker of his conversation with Dr. Blackburn, and Shrader straight away informed New Albany's mayor, Morris McDonald, who in turn summoned Chief of Police Stonecipher. The pair promptly decided to lay a trap for the grave robbers. Stonecipher detailed Officers Hennessey and Cannon to nab the thieves, and when the two officers reported to Shrader in the cemetery office, the Johnson brothers sat talking with the sexton. No one mentioned if the brothers had been summoned there or if they came regarding business about their brother's internment, but when the duo heard about the plan to steal their brother's body, wild horses could not have kept the pair from being a part of any plan to capture the ghouls. Hopper, a close friend of Pierce, and Deeble volunteered to assist the officers, and the six men, armed with twelve-gauge double-barreled shotguns loaded with .00 buckshot, entered the cemetery shortly after dark.

Four hours later, the six struggled to maintain their vigil in the inclement conditions. Shortly after the bells from nearby St. Mary's chimed midnight, the storm's fury temporarily abated, and Nathaniel Johnson heard the creaky rumble of wagon wheels on cobblestoned pavement coming down Eighth Street. The wagon stopped at the gate closest to where he and his two comrades hid among the shadowy tombstones. The trio watched as one man left the wagon, leaving four others behind on the cart, and jumped the iron fence surrounding the cemetery. He walked to Johnson's fresh grave, took a few moments to scrutinize the surroundings and then walked back to the gate. Upon his return, three of the men dismounted from the flatbed wagon and, jumping the fence, joined their companion. The group then slowly strolled to the dead man's resting place. They hesitated only a moment, looking around one last time, and then turned to their dastardly task.

Gently setting aside the flowers strewn across the muddy earth, one of the ghouls thrust a shovel into the grave and began digging as the Johnson brothers, infuriated by the defilement of their brother's final resting place, prepared to stop the desecration. Just as they began to move from concealment, the digging stopped and the robbers engaged in a somewhat heated debate. The brothers and Deeble could only make out a few of the hastily whispered words but later agreed that what they'd heard sounded like an argument. After a couple minutes of this intense and whispered debate, the group of thieves left Johnson's grave and headed in single file down the darkened lane toward Pierce's grave.

When the four fiends drew abreast of where the guards hid, the wet and angry men threw off their protective canvas camouflage and ordered the group to "THROW UP YOUR HANDS!" All of the robbers obeyed with the exception of one. Eighteen-year-old George Brown, a teenager described as having "one of the most villainous faces one would find in a day's travel" and an assistant janitor of the Kentucky School of Medicine, unsuccessfully tried to take advantage of the initial confusion to sneak off in the darkness, but as the teen tried to make his getaway, a shot rang out in the darkness and Brown's chest exploded in a mess of blood, flesh and gore, the steel pellets literally ripping his heart from his chest.

Deeble and the Johnson brothers later testified that the teenager had produced a concealed pistol when ordered to stop, and in fact a pistol was found within reach of the corpse (though the witnesses claimed Brown held tightly to the weapon). But people intent on shooting someone don't usually turn their backs on their intended victims, and the blast that killed eighteen-year-old George Brown hit him in the back just under his left shoulder blade.

The gun that fired the shot that killed Brown had been close enough to the young man that, when discharged, the shot passed entirely through the body and held together enough to leave "a hole as large as a saucer." All six of the men guarding the two graves claimed they never fired a single shot and left the cemetery with the same number of shells with which they had entered the burial ground, and no one was ever charged—or credited—

with the killing of George Brown. Deeble and the Johnson brothers claimed the shot that killed Brown must have come from an unseen accomplice of the robbers, though why the unseen shooter would have shot one of his companions and not targeted one of the men confronting his friends escapes me. How the shooter could have gotten so close to the victim without being seen by anyone is also a mystery.

The man left on the wagon, believed to have been Dr. Graham, also of the medical school, hastily fled with the vehicle upon hearing the shot that killed Brown but abandoned the wagon when it sank up to its axle hubs in the mud on Eleventh Street. The wagon was taken to Gwin's stable, and the man was never positively identified. The three remaining villains, two white men and one black man, raised their arms and surrendered another pistol and a hatchet but refused to identify themselves. The two white prisoners requested that the authorities contact the Louisville law firm of Jewett and Jewett to represent them and then refused to speak another word. Their African American accomplice didn't ask for any representation. He most likely couldn't afford any.

Taken to the Floyd County Jail on the northeast corner of State and Spring Streets, the jailers put the trio in separate cells. Word about the attempted robbery and subsequent arrest of the offenders spread quickly through New Albany that stormy Saturday night, and an angry crowd soon gathered outside the jail. Boisterous and angry drunks circulated among the mob of irate citizenry, demanding that the perpetrators face justice at the end of a rope. Many in the crowd agreed, and even those not present that night thought a proper hanging was in order.

When the two doctors later complained of the rough treatment they had received at the hands of the New Albany authorities, Josiah Gwin, editor of the *New Albany Public Press*, addressed their complaints in his paper:

> *Instead of being arrested and their necks protected, these infernal scoundrels should have been shot to death in their tracks in the cemetery they desecrated. They went there deliberately and in cold blood at the hour of midnight to commit a most foul and detestable crime, and yet because of arrest and protection from the just and righteous indignation of the entire people and mob violence, they whimper and complain of rough usage.*

Most of Gwin's readers agreed with the editor, with some notable exceptions: the doctors of New Albany, as well as several prominent members of the community, among them C.P. Cook, E.P. Easely, J.L. Stewart, E.B. Scribner, James K. Marsh, M.Z. Stannard and C.L. Jewett. The physicians in New Albany understood that any medical school needs a reliable and steady supply of corpses for the dissection labs. They publicly argued that medical students simply could not properly master human anatomy without time spent cutting up actual cadavers and/or parts of said cadavers. One writer claimed in a letter to the *New Albany Tribune* that the Louisville medical community had taken oaths not to use bodies, white or black, from Kentucky under penalty of dismissal from the faculty, but it remained at liberty to use whatever corpses it could procure from the burial grounds of southern Indiana.

At approximately nine o'clock the next morning, attorney Charles L. Jewett arrived to represent them. After talking to his clients, he advised them to say nothing further to anyone beyond acknowledging their presence in the cemetery the previous night.

Their lawyer identified the two white men as forty-five-year-old Dr. W.E. Grant, demonstrator of anatomy at the Kentucky School of Medicine, and thirty-five-year-old Dr. Blackburn, his assistant. Their African American companion was identified as forty-five-year-old William Mukes, the head janitor of the school. The *New Albany Public Press* described Dr. Grant, a lifelong bachelor, as "a fine looking man…well known and highly regarded in Louisville. He is a partner to Dr. E.R. Palmer and is connected with the Kentucky School of Medicine. From his appearance, one would think him the last person to be engaged in such hellish business as he was caught in last night." The paper reported that Blackburn told his wife when he left his house that stormy night that he was going to make a professional call and that she was unaware of his whereabouts until she read about the incident in the *Louisville Courier Journal* the following morning.

The Floyd County Grand Jury indicted all three men on two counts: one for attempting to rob a grave and the other for conspiring to commit a felony. According to Indiana law at the time the crimes occurred:

> *Any person who shall, without due process of law or the consent of the surviving husband or wife or next of kin of the deceased or of the person*

*having control of such grave, open any grave for the purpose of taking there-
from any such dead body or any part thereof buried therein, or anything
Interred therewith, shall be deemed guilty of a felony and upon conviction
thereof shall be imprisoned in the state prison for not less than three years
or more than ten years.*

The penalty for conspiring to commit a felony fixed the punishment at a fine of not more than $5,000 and imprisonment in the state prison for no less than two months or for more than ten years.

Another, even bigger, lynch mob gathered outside the jail that day, and to prevent any possible harm coming to the threesome, the police moved the men to the Indiana State Reformatory in Jeffersonville.

The next day, the trio was formally arraigned in court in New Albany and then made bail and was released. That was the last time any of the men appeared in court in New Albany. Attorney Jewett had their trial moved to Clark County, and the case was postponed several times. During this period, a battle raged between the New Albany paper and the Louisville papers. The Louisville paper defended the actions of the doctors and their accomplices, while the New Albany paper clamored for their imprisonment—or worse! Interestingly, after an article announcing the last postponement, Mr. Gwin never made another mention of the incident.

I looked through two years' worth of the *New Albany Public Press* trying to determine the outcome of the trial but could find nothing in the paper regarding the whole affair. I began to suspect that perhaps the men had been acquitted, and Gwin simply couldn't stand the thought of announcing the news. I had about given up on uncovering the result when an e-mail from a friend, Mrs. Barbara Ann Guyton Ziegenmeyer, supplied me with the answer.

The story made the news all over the country, and my friend discovered two articles, one in the *Aberdeen Daily News* and the other in the *Chicago Herald*, which solved the mystery. The jury acquitted the men after ten hours of deliberation. According to the *Herald*, "The verdict was obtained on a technicality. It was shown that the defendants had not even touched the earth of the graves and therefore it was alleged that they had committed no crime."

One interesting item came to light during the proceedings. Reports surfaced disputing Deeble's claim that he'd reported the offer made to him by Dr. Blackburn out of a sense of civic duty. The charge was made that the sexton's right-hand man had only reported the incident because Blackburn either wouldn't offer more money for the dirty deed or Deeble was protecting the consortium of physicians to whom he'd sold more than fifty corpses in the past few years. Deeble quite obviously disputed the reports and was never charged with the crime, but no one has ever opened a single grave to find out if the body buried there remains, for as one New Albanian claimed, "I buried my daughter there recently, and if her grave is opened and is found empty, I fear madness would be the result."

There's another interesting twist contrary to the accepted findings. The shot that killed Brown came from behind the young man, yet if he was where the sworn testimony of the six guards claimed, then he was within a few short steps of running smack into the solid stone wall of the Brigg family tomb, which most likely would have stopped him just as surely as the shotgun blast did, but without such lethal results. The description of the wound, the proximity of the weapon when fired and the evidence of the direction followed by the fatal shot could lead one to believe that the young African American was murdered in a fit of heated vengeance.

Finally, if you care to visit the cemetery today, you can see where the gore from Brown's torn body ended up. The Briggs vault still shows the scars from where the pellets hit the tomb.

# MOMMY DEAREST

Early in the evening of Tuesday, July 24, 1973, two New Albany police officers pulled up to 3131 Beacon Drive in New Albany. The patrolmen needed to notify Alicine and Eldon "Huggy" Marshall that the authorities in nearby Washington County held their sixteen-year-old son Fritz and his companion, fifteen-year-old Steven R. Mack of Hammond, in the county jail on theft charges for stealing a boat in nearby Salem, Indiana.

No one answered the door that steamy summer night, and when two different officers, Patrolman Mike Culwell and Sergeant Sam Sarkisan, returned to the home shortly after 10:00 a.m. the following day, they detected a sickly sweet smell emanating from the home. Searching around the outside of the house, they noticed all the windows and doors were closed and locked. Familiar with the nauseating aroma and suspecting foul play, the officers requested and received permission from police headquarters to force entry into the home. When they opened the front door, the fetid aroma emanating from the un-air-conditioned and closed-up home assaulted them like a punch to the face. Covering their mouths against the revolting stench, the pair cautiously explored the darkened rooms in the tiny ranch house.

They saw dried blood in every room, and the putrid smell of decaying flesh reeked in the stale air. The aroma grew more intense as they slowly walked down the hallway toward the pair of bedrooms on either side of the hall, but neither man saw a body in either of the tiny rooms. They went back to the living room, and Sarkisan, the senior of the two, told his partner, "Be quiet for a minute. Listen." At first Culwell didn't hear anything in the silent house…and then the junior officer heard what his partner wanted him to hear. When Sarkisan saw the look of disgust and recognition on Culwell's face, he nodded his head and said, "Flies."

The buzzing grew louder as they followed the sound back down the hallway to the bedroom on the left. Culwell's eyes had adjusted to the gloomy interior of the home, and this time when he peeked into the murky gloom of the poorly lit room, he saw a moving black blanket of hundreds, if not thousands, of flies atop a lump in the bed he hadn't noticed on his first quick survey. Sarkisan grabbed a corner of the mattress and directed his partner to grab the other. When the pair gingerly lifted the mattress amid a swarm of thousands of disturbed flies, they found the decomposing body of Alicine Marshall. The bedclothes wrapping the body moved from the squirming mass of maggots under the bloody cloth. Someone had wrapped her body in the sheets and then stuffed the grisly package between the mattress and box springs.

The officers quickly backed out of the room and sealed off the crime scene before calling in their gruesome discovery to police headquarters. An ambulance transported Mrs. Marshall's body to the Floyd Memorial Hospital on State Street in New Albany, where the county coroner, Dr. Daniel Cannon, performed an autopsy on the corpse. Dr. Cannon determined that though she'd fought her attacker, her assailant had managed to inflict seventeen stab wounds on her with a household butcher knife approximately six inches long. Dr. Cannon further announced that Alicine Marshall died from severe shock and bleeding sometime within the past forty-eight to seventy-two hours.

Officials at the Washington County Jail immediately notified her son, Fritz, who, to their amazement, admitted that he and young Mack had killed his mother in a fit of rage on Saturday night, July 21, 1973. Though appalled by the brutality of the crime, Fritz's confession really didn't surprise Culwell. A few years before murdering his mother, Marshall had killed several baby ducks at the home. His actions had so frightened Alicine, normally an overly protective mother quick to blame others for her son's behavior, that she called the police. Culwell was working in the juvenile section of the department then, and Fritz's bizarre act introduced the officer to the twisted teen.

Fritz and Stephen killed Alicine during the evening of my thirteenth birthday. I spent that night in my grandmother's home on Hickory Grove, and while the demented teens slowly tortured Alicine Marshall to death, I slept safe and comfortable less than fifty yards away. The next day, I celebrated my birthday, along with the visit of my California cousins Jack and Hermaline Schindler and their three children. The back of the Marshall home, including the bedroom where Alicine rapidly decomposed in the heat, is visible from the lot where I played and celebrated that day. As we ate cake and homemade ice cream, the flies feasted and mated on her mutilated corpse, and the thought that some of those I shooed from my plate might have recently dined on Alicine's rotted flesh that hot day in late July still creeps me out.

I'd known Fritz for about four years at the time he murdered his mother. I first met him in the summer of 1969, a year after my grandparents moved from their older bungalow on Morton Avenue in New Albany to their more elegant and spacious home on Hickory Grove. My friend Dana (who visited his grandmother's home across the street from my grandparents' house about as much as I visited mine) introduced us. I thought Fritz was kind of a jumpy kid. And if the story that soon made the rounds in the neighborhood is true, then Fritz had every right to be what the detectives on those cop shows in the '80s, when describing someone nervously and purposefully avoiding eye contact or switching their weight from foot to foot—or both—called "hinky."

Not long after our initial contact, I didn't see Fritz riding his bike around the neighborhood at his usual break-neck speed. I didn't see him riding his bike at any speed. In fact, I didn't see him at all. When I asked Dana why, he told me that Fritz had wanted to play football for his junior high school team that fall, but when he approached his mother about getting a physical so he could join the team, she refused. I know more than a few mothers are initially quite hesitant to let their sons participate in such a violent and often times bloody sport. They become practically paralyzed by fear at the thought of their sweet little boys slammed to the ground and trampled into sticky purplish pulp by the feet of some hulking brute twice the size of their dear little boys. I'm a parent myself and therefore understand that their rejection of the game is a natural reaction. It's a mother's instinct to protect her children from harm, but what Dana told me next makes what happened so shocking an act.

Dana claimed Fritz kept insisting that his mother sign the papers allowing him to play until Alicine finally snapped. The rumor that spread amongst at least us kids in the neighborhood that summer claimed that when Alicine snapped, she snapped Fritz's leg bones, ensuring that he wasn't going to play any football that year and ending the discussion once and for all. He couldn't get out of bed, so there wasn't any reason for him to bother her anymore about playing football, and she could finally have some peace and quiet.

I have nothing to verify that this actually happened. I never saw Fritz on crutches, but then I never saw Fritz at all until the early winter of 1980, and a lot had transpired between our last meeting and our unexpected reunion in the living room of my mother's house. We'd barely known each other the last time we'd talked, and now he was a member of my family. When Huggy married my stepfather's mother, Fritz became my step-uncle. I'm still not sure how I felt about the connection considering exactly what had happened in the intervening years since last we'd met.

Fritz's father, Huggy, probably wasn't home much that summer as Fritz continued to pester and annoy Alicine. If he had been, maybe we wouldn't know anything about any of them. A small, quiet man who kept mostly to himself and enjoyed drinking beer until he achieved a state of smiling, happy oblivion when off work, Huggy made his living as an engineer (really just a fancy title for a mechanic) on a tugboat on the Ohio and Mississippi Rivers. As a young sailor, he'd been in on many of the amphibious landings made by the Marine Corps during the deadly island-hopping campaign against the Imperial Japanese military, naval and air forces in the Pacific during World War II. Huggy piloted the landing craft that carried the U.S. Marine infantrymen from the transport ships through the hail of gunfire and artillery shells to the landing beaches. Every so often, when he was semi-drunk—but not enough to pass out just yet—he'd talk about his experiences.

Unfortunately, I didn't discover this until not long before he suffered the onset of Alzheimer's disease, and so I missed many of his stories. However, I'll never forget the ones he shared with me over beers in his kitchen one night.

I never met Alicine, but from what I gathered listening to the women of the neighborhood talk when they thought I wasn't listening, and in later conversations with family members who did know her, she wasn't the most pleasant person. Some whispered she'd had some mental problems, but I have no idea if the woman did or didn't, and I still don't to this day. I didn't even know her name until researching this story. I don't know how Alicine and Huggy met, though I did hear through my family that Fritz might not even have really been Huggy's son, that Alicine had gotten pregnant back in a time when single young women did *not* get that way, not if they expected to ever live a respectable life and marry a decent man. It was one thing to wed a war widow with another man's child, but few men would ever say "I do" to a woman who had already been with someone else. I remember hearing through the family that Huggy agreed to marry her in order to preserve her dignity and public standing in the tiny town of Palmyra, Indiana, where they both grew up and lived at the time of her "unfortunate incident." I'm sure she had no idea then how truly unfortunate her pregnancy would prove.

Huggy married my step-grandmother a few years after the brutal death of his first wife. He usually worked on the boat for most of the year. Most of the men and women I've known who worked on the powerful river tugs stay on the boats for a month before enjoying two weeks off at the end of their tours. Though I'm sure the times vary from company to company and from position to position within the companies, Huggy only made it home about twice a year. He enjoyed his life as an engineer on the water, keeping the huge diesels humming and moving the massive loads the barges carry upstream and down. Perhaps his passion for life on the river kept him on the water for longer periods than the average deckhand, but we often joked behind his and my step-grandmother's backs that he probably had another family he spent time with somewhere along the Mississippi or one of its backwaters instead of coming home to our kooky family and all its troubles and issues.

What I've uncovered leads me to believe the Marshall home was not a happy one that summer of 1968, and this may account for why Huggy spent so little time there.

By the summer of 1973, Alicine apparently had endured enough of Fritz and his strange behavior. She sent him to the Father Gibault School for Boys in Terre Haute, Indiana. Among the many programs the school offers to troubled children is a psychiatric residential treatment program. The program, designated the PRTF, is, according to the school's current website, "designed to provide a secure, stable environment to youth who require 24-hour secure care and need stabilization." PTRF is "suitable for youth who are not responding to lower levels of care." The school provides locked, secure living units for its young patients,

> *who may be experiencing difficulties in the following areas: family functioning or social relatedness, sub acute or chronic illness, self care difficulties, and/or impaired safety such as threat to harm others. Developed for youth who have affective disorders, ADD, oppositional defiance, conduct disorder, sexual/emotional/physical abuse, anxiety disorder and adjustment disorders, the treatment plans are developed to meet individual needs and are reviewed weekly by the treatment team.*

Fritz met Steven Mack during his stay at Father Gibault's school, and eventually the unruly teens decided to leave the school's strictly disciplined environment, which they did in late June or early July 1973. Soon after fleeing the institution, the pair stole a truck and made their way south to Prattville, Alabama, where the local police soon arrested them.

On Saturday morning, July 21, Alicine flew to Prattville. Huggy had left earlier that week to return to his job on the river, and he didn't know of his wife's plan to retrieve Fritz. I don't know if she bonded the boys out or if the local police dropped the charges against the pair of juvenile delinquents, but I do know that Alicine, Fritz and Steven took a bus back to Louisville and then a cab to the Marshall home on Beacon Avenue.

The atmosphere remained tense through the early evening hours as the trio argued about the boys' plan to go to California. Alicine informed Steven that he'd be returning to Father Gibault's school as soon as possible, and the environment in the house became as heated as the hot and humid weather that fateful evening as the quarrel intensified. Sometime after midnight, while the argument continued in the kitchen, one of the boys (it was never determined which one) grabbed a butcher knife and stabbed Alicine in the chest.

She fought her attacker, who dropped the weapon, but the other boy picked up the knife and continued to stab Alicine as she ran into the other room, desperate to escape the assault. Unable to avoid the deadly blows or make her way to the front door, she turned and fled down the hall, receiving several more wounds in her back and neck, her blood spattering across the walls, ceilings and floor. She finally ran into her bedroom and either collapsed on her bed or the boys forced her there as they struck the last fatal blows.

Accounts vary as to the number of wounds Alicine suffered. When I first heard the story, the boys had allegedly stabbed her over one thousand times, but those stories turned out to be nothing more than the exaggeration that usually accompanies such gruesome tales. The *New Albany Tribune* reported that Dr. Cannon stated she'd suffered seventeen stab wounds, but later accounts in the paper placed the number as high as twenty-five. No matter how many wounds she suffered, no one blow caused her death. Instead, according to the autopsy report, Alicine Marshall expired due to shock and hemorrhaging caused by the injuries she suffered.

Fritz and Steven wrapped her body in the bloody bedsheets and then put her between the mattress and box springs. Though no detailed account exists, we can assume the boys cleaned the blood off themselves and then closed the windows in the home. We do know that they gathered some clothing, grabbed Alicine's purse and then left in her car, driving north on Interstate Highway 65. As they drove along the interstate, one of the pair searched through her purse and removed what they needed before tossing the purse out somewhere near Austin, Indiana.

Turning off the highway, the pair proceeded on back roads to Salem, Indiana. A violent thunderstorm raged that deadly night, the accompanying heavy downpour turning the normally small creeks in the area into raging torrents that overflowed onto the roadways. The murderous duo soon found itself trapped on a tiny bit of ground between two flooded areas. Forced to desert the car, the pair stole a boat to cross one swollen tributary. Once across, the two boys abandoned the stolen craft and fled on foot, spending the next two nights on farms in the Salem area before their capture on Tuesday, July 24, by local authorities. The sheriff transported the pair to the Washington County Jail at Salem, Indiana, and charged the boys with the theft of the watercraft. The authorities in Salem notified the New Albany

Police Department, which then proceeded to the Marshall home to inform Mrs. Marshall of her son's arrest and detention that night.

When confronted by the authorities later that day regarding the murder, both boys quickly confessed and signed statements outlining the sequence of events that had led up to that deadly Saturday night. Transported to the Floyd County Jail in New Albany, the teens appeared before Judge Paul J. Tegart on Monday, July 30, 1973. New Albany Police chief Thomas Downs prepared the affidavit, which brought the pair before the court. The affidavit claimed in part, "On July 22, in the County of Floyd, Marshall and Mack then and there unlawfully, feloniously and maliciously and with premeditated malice killed a human being, to wit, Alicine K. Marshall, by stabbing her with a sharp instrument inflicting a mortal wound upon her from which mortal wound Alicine K. Marshall died."

Fritz's father retained former city judge Basil Lorch Jr. to defend his son, but when Judge Tegart asked Steven Mack if he had any representation, the youngster simply shook his head no. The judge then asked Mack if he could afford to hire a lawyer, and Mack said he couldn't.

"Where are you from?" the judge asked.

Mack answered, "From Hammond."

"Has anybody been down here to see you since you've been incarcerated?"

"No. Nobody."

Joseph E. Earl, the prosecuting attorney, informed the court that the grand jury had been called in for the following day and stated, "I want the grand jury to take up this matter before pursuing it further."

Judge Tegart agreed with prosecutor Earl, saying, "There will be no pleas accepted at this time." The judge then declared that the case presented a rare circumstance in that two youths under the age of eighteen faced a capital crime. Usually, a youngster charged in a less than capital case was reprimanded to the custody of the juvenile branch of the court, but Judge Tegart noted that this case would go before the grand jury the following day.

The pair returned to the custody of the Floyd County Jail, where the boys remained until their separate trials, scheduled for January and February 1974. On Wednesday, December 5, 1973, a hearing took place before Judge Tegart to determine if Fritz Marshall had the mental capacity to understand the nature of the charges against him and determine if he was capable of assisting in his defense. Fritz, described as a "very tall and slim youth, with heavy black hair and…shell-rim glasses," wore an orange and black turtleneck sweater in his brief appearance in the courtroom. Judge Tegart ordered the teen from the room before Dr. Vicdan Sendal of the Southern Indiana Mental Health Center gave her testimony.

In her report, the doctor claimed that though "he was suffering from a personality disturbance" and had been on medication at different times, as well as given a shock treatment, her testing revealed "no psychosis." Both the defense and the prosecution questioned Dr. Sendal regarding her examination of Fritz. When asked by the prosecution, "In your opinion, is he [Fritz] able to understand the nature of the case against him and to assist in his defense?" the doctor replied, "I believe so."

Despite Dr. Sendal's testimony, on the following Friday, December 7, Judge Tegart agreed with the defense team that the opinion of a second physician should be sought. The defense was disappointed when, two weeks later, that physician also testified that Fritz was competent to stand trial.

Steven Mack never received a psychiatric examination prior to the trial, a joint affair for Fritz and Steven set for January 14, 1974. The court ordered the pair held without bond. Before the trial date, the defense got the court to agree on two separate trials.

On Friday, January 4, 1974, ten days before Steven Mack's trial on a charge of first-degree murder for stabbing to death Alicine Marshall, his court-appointed attorney arranged a plea bargain that the state accepted. Mack pleaded guilty to a reduced charge of second-degree murder. The pre-sentence investigation took one week to complete, and on Friday, January 11, 1974, Judge Tegart sentenced sixteen-year-old Steven Mack to fifteen to twenty-five years in prison for his part in the horrific homicide. Mack was immediately transported to the Plainfield, Indiana diagnostic center to determine in which prison he should serve his sentence. The unexpected plea bargain changed the date for Fritz's trial, which had been scheduled for the following Monday, January 14. The new date was set for Wednesday, February 20, 1974.

The day of the trial dawned sunny and bright with highs expected in the mid-fifties. Fritz, "a tall, thin, bespectacled boy" exhibiting "a tendency toward nervousness, clasping and unclasping his hands, streaking his fingers through his long hair," appeared before Judge Tegart with his attorney, Basil Lorch Jr., and Huggy. Lorch began by reminding the court that his client had previously pleaded guilty to the charge of first-degree murder. "There has been much consideration given to this case," the lawyer said. "With the court's permission, we would like to change our plea to the amended charge of second-degree murder."

When the prosecution accepted the request, which Judge Tegart immediately approved, Lorch turned to Huggy and asked, "You understand what this means? Could mean imprisonment?" Huggy replied that he understood, and Lorch repeated the question to Fritz, who, in a clear and steady voice, replied that he also understood the possible ramifications of his plea.

Judge Tegart then interrupted and asked both father and son if anyone had made them any promises concerning the plea bargain. Both said that no one had offered them any deals for the plea. Officials then returned Fritz to the county lockup to await the results of the pre-sentence investigation. Huggy slowly walked with his head down toward the elevator.

Less than a week later, Fritz Marshall was shocked when the court imposed a life sentence on him for participating in his mother's murder. Though the court had imposed a fairly lenient sentence (soft in light of the horrendous nature of their joint crime) on his accomplice, Steven Mack, Judge Tegart threw the proverbial book at Fritz. The young killer was immediately removed from the courtroom and soon after taken to the Plainfield diagnostic center, where, after a brief stay, Fritz Marshall was sent to the Indiana State Reformatory at Pendleton, Indiana, to serve out his life sentence.

This is where the murderous tale should have ended—with justice served and both killers locked away for a long time. However, neither Fritz nor Steven would serve their entire sentences. On Thursday, August 26, 1976, as the nation still celebrated its 200th anniversary and the world's first known case of the Ebola virus appeared in Yambuku, Zaire, Steven Mack and his new legal team again appeared before Judge Tegart. Consisting of Indianapolis attorney Miles Stanton, from the office of the attorney general of Indiana, and two lawyers from New Albany, James Bourne and Michael McDonalds, Mack's legal team requested that his conviction be overturned because, they claimed, their client hadn't been properly informed of his rights prior to his accepting the plea agreement reached between him and the state.

Joseph Earl, the man who had prosecuted Mack in the first trial and accepted the plea bargain, claimed that Mack had been advised that in pleading guilty to the reduced charge he was foregoing his right to trial by jury, his right to call any and all witnesses and his right to face his accusers.

Earl claimed he made all of this clear to Mack prior to his acceptance of the plea bargain.

Mack's defense team responded, "We have only to go on what the record shows. While it shows that he [Mack] waived these rights, it doesn't show specifically that he was told what these rights are."

Judge Tegart denied the appeal, but a little more than a year later, the Indiana Court of Appeals agreed with the defense team and overturned Steven Mack's conviction. The state decided not to retry him, and Mack walked free after he'd served less than four years for his part in the brutal slaying.

A little more than a year later, Fritz appeared back in Floyd County in the courtroom of Judge David W. Crumbo. Stanton presented a plea of agreement reached between the attorney general's office and the state that would terminate the remainder of Marshall's life sentence. The attorney general's office based its claim on the fact that because Mack's conviction had been overturned, the remainder of Fritz's sentence should be vacated. The state simply didn't want to retry both men.

Amazingly, Judge Crumbo accepted the new plea bargain, agreeing that since Mack's conviction had been overturned, Marshall's should also be reversed. The judge, claiming he wanted to do what was in the murderous youth's best interests, called several witnesses to the court, including Huggy and his new bride, my step-grandmother, Wanda Marshall. Huggy claimed he would try to get Fritz a job at American Commercial Barge Lines, where the father currently worked, and Wanda said she'd do what she could about taking Fritz into her home. The judge listened carefully to all of the testimony and then decided that Fritz shouldn't be released until after he'd undergone a period of rehabilitation in a course at the Pendleton penitentiary. Stephen Beardsley, the prosecutor at the time, noted that Fritz would be eligible for parole soon anyway. So, after completing the course at the penitentiary, Fritz Marshall walked away a free man. Both youngsters served less than seven years for the brutal murder of Alicine Marshall.

I have no idea where Steven Mack landed or where he is today. I've also lost contact with Fritz. The last I heard, he'd married Thea Graham in June 1981 and not long afterward moved to Texas, where he found religion and became heavily involved in a local church. Maybe his newly found religion will serve him well in the afterlife.

However, if I were him, I wouldn't count on it. I doubt Satan is as forgiving as the Indiana judicial system.

The federal government erected a magnificent stone post office on the site of the salt lick where the Native Americans quartered Sullivan. This photo shows the Spring Street façade. *Courtesy of the Indiana Room.*

Before merchant Elias Ayres had this building constructed in 1825, Frederick Nolte operated a bakery from his log home on the site. John Dahmen killed Nolte here in the city's first official murder.

An intoxicated Thomas Moore killed his equally drunken lifelong friend Albert Sinex on a rainy July afternoon in 1868 in the Belvidere Saloon, which once stood on this corner.

Berry Gwin operated a stable on this corner in 1868. Gwin and a partner also operated an undertaking business here. His daughter, Elizabeth, and her husband, Thomas Moore, lived on the property.

The Sinex family mausoleum, built to accommodate forty-two caskets, approximately thirty of which are currently occupied, is one of the oldest vaults in the Fairview Cemetery. The first interment in the structure, sealed on December 4, 1978, took place shortly after the tomb's construction in 1850.

Former New Albany mayor Charles B. McLinn said of Easely, one of the city's most prominent and well-respected physicians, after the doctor's death on August 2, 1935: "I never knew a man so thoroughly versed in Shakespeare as Dr. Easely. He always had an apt quotation from the English poet in illustration of a point." I wonder which of the Bard's words Easely quoted when he found Jacob Ritter still alive. *Courtesy of the Indiana Room.*

Originally called the Northern Burial Grounds, the city's second oldest cemetery's name was changed to Fairview in 1896. The tall monument marks the grave of Washington C. DePauw. The lake is long gone. *Courtesy of the Indiana Room.*

This map, which appeared in the *New Albany Tribune* on February 25, 1890, illustrates the positions of the individuals, both dead and alive, involved in the event.

surroundings. Going lurther up the main avenue, he met Deeble and requested that the graves of both Pierce and Thomas Johnson be pointed out to him. Deeble thought he was probably a friend of the dead men, and did as he was requested. Imagine his surprise when the stranger, who by the way was afterward found to be Dr. J. T. Blackburn, exhibited a large roll of bills, and tendered Deeble $2 in payment, as he said, for the trouble of walking 200 yards with him. He cautioned Deeble to keep quiet and he would give him the whole plan, which he did. He stated that the bodies were wanted by the Louisville doctors, and that the graves were to be robbed last night, and promised Deeble a $20 bill if he would aid in the work. Deeble seemed to heartily indorse the plan, and Dr. Blackburn appeared satisfied, for he scaled the Eighth street fence of the cemetery

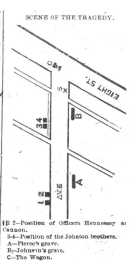

SCENE OF THE TRAGEDY.

1 2—Position of Officers Hennessey and Cannon.
3-4—Position of the Johnson brothers.
A—Pierce's grave.
B—Johnson's grave.
C—The Wagon.

A MISTAKEN REPORT.

Stone contractors Diebold, Crumbo and Melcher built this mausoleum for John Briggs in the summer of 1874. On July 25, 1874, the *New Albany Daily Ledger* claimed that the vault "reflects great credit upon their skill and taste as workers in stone, as well as upon the liberality of Mr. Briggs, who thus adorns and beautifies our magnificent city of the dead." A blast from a twelve-gauge shotgun killed eighteen-year-old George Brown here on February 24, 1890.

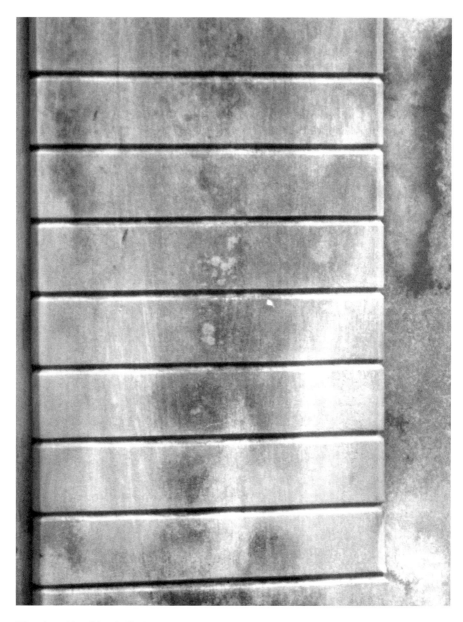

The nine .32-caliber balls that removed George Brown's heart from his chest marred the magnificent stone work of the Briggs family vault after exiting the young man's body. The original contractors repaired the damage not long after the killing.

Fritz Marshall and Stephen Mack murdered Marshall's mother, Alicine Marshall, in this unassuming three-bedroom ranch-style home on the night of July 21, 1973. The blood evidence showed that the deadly duo assaulted Mrs. Marshall in every room in the house.

Large strings of huge freight cars pulled by massive locomotives weren't New Albany's only "Wheels of Death." Several victims died underneath a streetcar similar to the one in this undated photograph. *Courtesy of the Indiana Room.*

John Marrs Jr. is only one of several New Albanians killed on the tracks running down the middle of East Fifteenth Street. A freight train killed the ten-year-old near this spot on Thursday, September 29, 1887.

A backing train struck William Davidson near this spot. His head and other body parts ended up strewn between here and the middle of the intersection of the tracks and East Market Street in the background.

The graphic descriptions Gwin provided in his *New Albany Public Press* enthralled New Albanians from 1881 until his death in 1901. His readers devoured the gossip he printed as well. One warning to a married woman and a single man from "respectable families" to "go slow" led to the man's murder by the cuckold husband a little past noon on a hot July day in 1886 near the alley between East Third and Fourth Streets on Market Street.

Nicholas Bettinger watched in horror as a passing freight train struck and killed his friend John Williamson on January 16, 1919. Williamson walked east on the north side of these tracks.

Two passersby discovered bits and pieces of Henry Trunk's dismembered corpse scattered along these tracks in the predawn darkness of an April morning in 1886.

*Above*: Harry Dellinger, killed in a train accident, lies in state in the front room of his home. Most families typically held their deceased loved ones' funerals in their homes up until the mid-twentieth century. *Courtesy of the Indiana Room.*

*Left*: Enoch West worked on the first floor of James Forman's tea shop for more than a decade. He lived on the second floor and died by his own hand on the third.

*Right*: The friends and family of Enoch West placed this marker atop his grave not long after the clerk cut his own throat on the night of November 3, 1885.

*Below*: Built in the mid-1850s, this building has been the Central Hotel, the Windsor Hotel and the New Albany Inn, among other titles. Thousands of visitors, both famous and infamous, stayed in what was once New Albany's finest inn. Many deaths occurred in the hotel, including T.G. Gorman, who committed suicide on the third floor. At the time of this writing, the building is home to the Habana Blues Tapas Restaurant. *Courtesy of the Indiana Room.*

Distraught by the death of her son, Louisa Manor jumped through a second-floor
window of her in-laws' home in Xenia, Ohio, in 1885. Both her obituary and the
cemetery records list her as "Weda" Manor.

At seven thirty on Thanksgiving morning in 1937, Ruth Sinkhorn shot herself in the
stomach with her husband's .20-gauge shotgun in this house. She died at St. Edward's
Hospital twelve agonizing hours later.

After the death of his first wife, Lloyd Sinkhorn lived here in 1943 with his second wife, Helen, and his son, Jackie. Four months after the couple's marriage, Lloyd drowned in Silver Creek.

The citizen's group the New Albany Better Government Committee, led by Chamber of Commerce president Dudley Jewell, claimed that New Albany's gambling syndicate paid off most of these officers. *From left to right, front row*: Joe Wimp, Chief Ed Meyer and Mr. Cureton. *Back row*: Charles Schrader, unknown, unknown, unknown, Antford G. "Son" Capper, unknown, unknown, unknown, Guy Hosbash, unknown, unknown and Dewey Boyd. *Courtesy of the Indiana Room.*

New Albany mayor Raymond Jaegers committed suicide in his office in the courthouse in 1946, the same year a photographer snapped this picture of the building on the southeast corner of State and Spring Streets. *Courtesy of the Indiana Room.*

Five unidentified men pose in front of the offices of the W.H. McKay Insurance Company at what was then 23 East Main Street in this photograph taken in either 1886 or 1887. *Courtesy of the Indiana Room.*

Eight unidentified New Albanians posed near the city stables in this photograph from sometime around the turn of the twentieth century. *Courtesy of the Indiana Room.*

Two Floyd County officers practice with their firearms while a third officer observes on the shooting range in the basement of the old Floyd County Courthouse on the southeast corner of State and Spring Streets. *Courtesy of the New Albany Police Departmen.*

# Part II

# The Steel Wheels
# of Death

Before the coming of the railroads, America relied on steamboats to carry large numbers of people and products across the country. Though the paddle-wheelers carried their cargo up and down America's waterways faster than any other available method of transportation at the time, the inland steamers were limited as to where they could go. If no river route to one's intended destination existed, people either went by foot or relied on horse power to move themselves and their belongings. Tons of materials and supplies needed to transform untamed wilderness into civilized centers of commerce and trade would have been carried across the wide-open spaces by slow-moving wagons with limited carrying capacity without the advent of railroads. Our Manifest Destiny to expand from sea to shining sea would have taken much longer to fulfill without the railroads that enabled our young nation to develop much more quickly. America owes a great deal to those forward-thinking individuals who funded and built those steel ribbons upon which the rapidly growing country relied.

While our obligation to the railroads that opened up this great land is indeed large, much of that debt has been repaid in blood.

Most of us are aware of what happened when Casey Jones neglected to watch his speed, but the unwary engineer's death certainly isn't the only one associated with railroads. Thousands of Americans have died in train derailments and collisions. An untold number of railroad workers and others died when crushed between the massive cars in switchyards across the country, and since the advent of the automobile, thousands have died when they either ignored the flashing lights at a crossing or tried to beat a speeding train to the intersection. However, probably the single biggest cause of death involving trains occurs when people try to board a moving train, even a slow-moving one.

Trains have killed literally hundreds of New Albanians in all of the ways noted in the previous paragraph, especially in the switchyards in the city, but I have included here only those whose bodies the grinding steel wheels of death mangled and mauled.

## A Family Torn to Pieces

Sixteen-year-old Richard Marrs smiled as he walked north on East Ninth Street late in the afternoon of October 31, 1885. The crisp, clean air carried just the slightest hint of the coming winter chill, and the sun shining in the bright blue sky above him that Saturday warmed the teen as he contentedly strolled up the roadway's slight incline toward Main Street.

He'd just picked up his paycheck from his employer, and the money felt good in his pocket. For the past year, the industrious teenager had worked part time in the bottle house of the DePauw Glass Works, located on the east side of New Albany between the banks of the Ohio River and Main Street, and he genuinely enjoyed his job there. He especially liked the money he earned. Though he didn't have to, he often gave part of his wages to his father, New Albany city policeman John Marrs Sr., because he liked the thought that his contribution helped his family. He appreciated the hard, sometimes dangerous work his father did, and the youngster believed that every penny he gave helped his beloved family enjoy the good life they lived.

While his part in assisting his tightknit family made him feel like a man, a sensation he took pleasure in, he liked the fact that the hours he worked in the plant didn't interfere with his education. He took his schooling quite seriously, more so than many young men of his age, and he would not have worked at the factory if doing so had negatively impacted his studies. He also knew his devotion to his schooling set a good example for his younger siblings, especially seven-year-old John Jr.

# The Steel Wheels of Death

Little John adored his elder brother. He often emulated Richard's walk and speech and followed him around so much that people soon began asking Richard where his shadow had gone when John wasn't with him. Richard returned his little brother's admiration, allowing him to tag along when possible, and when earlier that day he'd told John he wouldn't be able to spend time with him that evening because he had plans to attend a Halloween party that night, he'd felt badly when he saw the tears well up in the child's adoring eyes.

Though sad he'd hurt his little brother's feelings, with his pockets full of money and anticipating a delightful evening with his friends, Richard Marrs was indeed a happy young man as he made his way toward the tracks of the Airline Accommodation Train at a little before four o'clock that beautiful fall day.

Normally, the thrifty teen walked to his family's residence at 218 West Market Street, but he probably thought riding the train would get him home sooner, thereby allowing him some play time with his little brother. No one will ever know what motivated Richard, because when the east bound train approached, moving along at its usual speed of about five miles per hour, the happy young man jumped aboard the slow-moving conveyance…and lost his footing, falling headfirst under the grinding steel wheels.

The unforgiving wheels crushed the unfortunate lad's head, completely flattening the back of his skull and literally mashing the left side of his body to a bloody pulp. The unrelenting assault crushed his left shoulder and split his left arm wide open, the bones in the limb broken into small fragments. The wheels continued mincing his battered body, splitting open his left leg from the hip down, shattering the bones and ripping off his left shoe.

Several men who witnessed the appalling accident removed his mangled corpse from the tracks. Someone notified Officer Marrs of the calamity that had befallen his oldest son, and when he arrived at the scene of the tragic mishap, he had his son's mutilated body carried to Shrader's funeral home. Deputy coroner W.L. Starr examined the body at Shrader's and determined that among the numerous injuries inflicted on the young man's body, Richard's neck was broken. We can only hope that the injury occurred when his head first hit the pavement, thereby rendering him, if not instantly dead, then at least insensible to the injuries that immediately followed his fall.

Starr found the death to be accidental. The coroner finished his work by handing the dead teen's wages for the week to the boy's parents—all $2.50.

Richard's funeral took place on Monday afternoon, November 2, 1885, in the family's home on Elm Street. The Marrses attended the Wesley Chapel Methodist Church, and the pastor of the church, Reverend A.R. Julian, conducted the service. When the funeral ended, Richard's body was buried in Plot 2, Range 14, Lot 26, in the Fairview Cemetery.

The family was naturally devastated by their loss, particularly John Jr. The lad found the loss of his older brother excruciating. He couldn't bear to hear anyone even mention Richard's name, but time heals all wounds, and young boys are often the quickest to recover from such tragedies. The heartbroken little boy soon put the tragedy behind him and resumed his normal activities. The rest of his family eventually did the same, the horror of that fall day in 1885 always in their memories but not in their minds as often as it had been in the days and weeks following the tragic accident.

By September 1887, tranquility had returned to the Marrs home on Market Street, the house once again a lively and vibrant home. John Sr. had been appointed to the post of chief of police, and his wife, no longer too overcome with grief to properly care for her family and her home, had returned to her normal self. The three Marrs children performed well in school. Following his deceased brother's example, John Jr. applied himself to his studies and became an outstanding student. As personable and likeable as his brother had been, he called most of the boys around his age in his neighborhood friends.

The youngsters liked to spend their hours out of school doing the things most boys their age enjoy doing in their free time. They swam and fished in the many creeks and ponds within walking distance of their neighborhood in the west end of the city and often ventured to the nearby Ohio River to frolic and play. When not taking advantage of the natural opportunities for play, the boys liked to play games like hoop and stick, blind man's bluff or fox and geese, and when inclement weather kept them indoors, they'd play checkers, or chess, or pickup sticks. But when the weather was right, not too hot and not too cold, John Marrs Jr. and his many friends played baseball.

About a quarter past three o'clock on the afternoon of Thursday, September 29, 1887, John Jr. and his friends headed for the baseball park on the east side of town after school. They walked on the tracks of the Louisville, New Albany & Ohio Railroad, which still run down the middle of East Fifteenth Street, moving out of the way when a freight train, consisting of seventeen cars and pulled by engine #50, began slowly backing down the track. When they got to the block between Elm and Oak Streets, John Jr., either bored or wanting to impress his friends, decided, almost unbelievably in light of what had happened to his older brother, to jump on the train for a ride. He jumped on the third car from the end, on the east side of the track. He rode the train for about twenty feet…and then lost his grip, falling underneath the train's murderous wheels.

Two of the freight cars passed over him, cutting off both his legs near the trunk of his body and partially disemboweling him. Despite his horrendous wounds, the young man didn't immediately die. Several witnesses to the accident, including his young comrades, gathered around the terribly mangled boy, astonished not only that he still lived despite his horrific injuries but also that he remained conscious and alert. He never uttered a cry, telling the onlookers his name and where he lived. He then asked that someone notify his mother of the accident. One of the bystanders, informing the horribly wounded lad that he couldn't possibly live but for a few more minutes, asked the dying youngster if he had any words he'd like to send to his parents.

"Yes," he slowly and calmly replied. "Tell ma and pa goodbye for me and to forgive me for anything wrong I have done."

The bystanders placed his mutilated body on a litter and carried the boy to a nearby house on Elm Street. For approximately the next forty-five minutes, the mortally wounded child continued to talk and answer any questions asked of him. After answering the last question posed to him, he closed his eyes and grew very still and quiet. Two minutes later, the last surviving son of police chief John Marrs and his wife died.

His maimed body was carried to Shrader's Funeral, and once again, Coroner Starr was called to examine the body. Like his brother's before him, his parents held their son's funeral in the family's residence. Numerous friends and neighbors attended the service, including the entire police force of New Albany, held at two o'clock on the afternoon of Saturday, September 30, 1887. Once again, Reverend A.R. Julian conducted the service. When the funeral ended, the young man's body was taken to the Fairview Cemetery and buried next to his brother's.

Mrs. Marrs never fully recovered from the horrible death of her last son. She died a couple of years later and was buried next to her boys. John Sr.

lost his position in the police force when a new mayor assumed office. When Marrs remarried a few years after his first wife's death, he and his new wife moved away from New Albany. Who could blame him for wanting to leave a town that held so many bad memories for him?

Curiously, despite the fact that by all accounts there was an enormous amount of love and respect shared in the Marrs household, no stone or marker memorializes either boy or their mother. Though it is possible that any stones that may once have marked the final resting place of the trio were lost due to vandalism (sadly, the cemetery has suffered several instances of such senseless damage in its long history), there is no indication that the concrete foundations upon which most tombstones stand ever existed on the site. The only indication of the final resting place of the mother and her two sons are the four plain stones that mark the boundaries of the family plot.

John Marrs Sr. was buried in the town to which he and his new bride moved after leaving the city where his wife and two sons lie buried. As far as anyone knows, he never returned to New Albany.

## UNDER THE WHEELS

William Davidson spent most of his adult life in New Albany. Five feet, eight inches tall with a dark complexion, the slightly built Davidson was kindhearted and friendly. He had a pleasant disposition and was a hardworking and honest man. His compassionate and sociable personality, combined with his strong work ethic and integrity, made him many friends in the city.

The outgoing sixty-four-year-old, partially deaf and slowly going blind, enjoyed spending time conversing with friends over a few beers. Every now and then, he'd have too many of the brews, but even on those rare occasions when he imbibed too much of the amber liquid, he was a happy drunk. Cruelty and meanness, whether drunk or sober, were just not in his nature.

Davidson spent a couple of hours in a local tavern near the intersection of Vincennes and Main Streets in the city's east end during the late afternoon hours of Monday, November 22, 1875, enjoying a beer or two with some of his buddies. As usual, they discussed local and national events, the conversation light and easy going. They played cards and probably talked about one of their friends who had recently been badly injured by a runaway wagon. A little after five o'clock, Davidson drained the remainder of his last beer, donned his coat and then headed for his home near Vincennes Street. Though he'd had a few beers during the two or three hours he'd spent in the small saloon, he had slowly sipped them, and none of those present, when later asked about his condition when he left the bar that chilly fall day, thought him intoxicated. He might have had a wee bit of a buzz, but he wasn't drunk by any means when he headed out the door.

His injured friend's house stood between the bar and Davidson's small house, and William stopped by his pal's home to see if the wounded man needed anything. He spent about thirty minutes with his buddy, making sure he had everything he needed for the night. Before he left, he asked his friend if he might borrow a shovel, and the injured man agreed. Content that his friend was comfortable and settled in for the evening, Davidson grabbed the tool he'd asked to borrow and headed out into the now dark night for the comfort of his own home and family.

William often took a shortcut to his home down the tracks of the Louisville, New Albany & Chicago Railroad that ran a short distance between Main and Market Streets. Though the evening was dark and his eyesight poor, he'd walked this way hundreds of times without any problems and most likely wasn't overly concerned that any harm would befall him this time. If only he'd known how wrong his assumption was.

As the happily buzzed and contented Davidson carefully made his way along the uneven roadway, a train consisting of a locomotive engine, five platform cars and one boxcar, the latter at the end of the string of cars, slowly backed down the tracks toward a junction with the line of the Jeffersonville, Madison & Indianapolis Railroad. Steve Hardin controlled the operation of the train and had earlier directed one of the yard workers to hang lights on the cars, especially on the back of the boxcar. The worker placed three lanterns on the platform cars but for some unknown reason neglected to place one on the rear of the boxcar as instructed. Hardin rode on the second car of the string.

As Davidson cautiously made his way in the darkness along the east side of the track, he heard someone shout, "Get out of the way!" Surprised, William looked up and saw the slowly approaching train, moving at a speed of about four miles an hour, approximately eight feet from him. The warning had come from Martin Welch, the brakeman, who, lantern in hand, had just stepped onto the rear car.

When the old man made a futile attempt to grab on to the boxcar, the now panicked Welch hollered, "Don't!" but the warning came too late. Davidson fell underneath the steel wheels. Welch felt the car run over the old man and frantically applied the brakes on the car, trying to stop the train, but his action only slowed the heavy string of cars. The brakeman then yelled to Hardin, "Man under the train!"

Hearing Welch's frightened call, Hardin turned and signaled toward the engine to stop the train. The train's fireman, James Ryves, looking out his side of the train, saw Hardin's signal and immediately told the engineer, J.W. Wheadon, to apply the brakes. Wheadon thought the bumps he'd just felt as the wheels passed over Davidson's body the result of the train passing over boards placed on the track. He applied the brakes, but stopping even a slow moving train takes time. By the time the train finally stopped, all of the cars had passed over Davidson, the engine coming to a halt atop what remained of his body.

The train dragged Davidson more than seventy-five feet. What remained of him ended up at a right angle to the track where the steel rails intersect Market Street, about fifteen feet from the west side of one of New Albany's landmark restaurants, Tommy Lancaster's.[7] His head, torn from his body, lay a little over forty feet south of the building. The wheels pressed both of his feet flat and crushed his legs. His blood covered the track for almost three hundred feet, the distance required for the train to come to a complete stop. The editor of the *New Albany Daily Ledger* described the ghastly spectacle in his paper the next day: "No one could gaze upon the scene without turning heart sick."

Bystanders gathered Davidson's mangled remains and took them to his residence less than a block away from the horrible accident. Today, any corpse so badly mutilated is generally presented to the family inside a locked casket, sparing them the horror of seeing their disfigured and decapitated loved one. Imagine the horror his family experienced when they saw Davidson's crumpled corpse come through their front door. According to the *Ledger* account, "The sorrowful anguish of the bereaved and destitute family would have melted the stoutest heart to pity."

News of the tragedy quickly spread through the city, and a crowd of people gathered at the home to get a glimpse of Davidson's mangled body.

Floyd County coroner E.L. Pennington conducted an investigation that night. The members of the coroner's jury gave the following verdict:

*After having heard the evidence and examined the body, we do find that deceased came to his death by being run over by a train belonging to the above named Railroad Company, and we, the jury, do further find that deceased came to his death through the neglect of officers and employees of said road to provide, and cause to be placed upon rear of said train above alluded to, proper signal lights. Given under our hands, this 22nd day of November, 1875.*
*George Watkins, Clerk*
*John W. Saunders,*
*James E. Unks,*
*William A. Manor,*
*Isaiah Sheldon,*
*Wesley Pierce.*

The railroad declared that Davidson's intoxication caused his death and not any neglect on its part. Furious at the company's claim, the *Ledger*'s editor asserted in his paper the day after the accident that William's kind heart had killed him, stating that if the loyal friend hadn't stopped to see to his friend's needs, "he would have reached his home before the passing train. The above is, perhaps, as true a statement of the matter as can be gained, and his last kindly act is proof positive that he was not intoxicated."

The family held William Davidson's funeral in his home the following day. They buried him in the Fairview Cemetery in Plot 2, Range 17, Lot 20, but no stone marks his final resting place. If a tombstone once stood guard over his remains, the monument is long gone. Though the company eventually settled with his family out of court for an undisclosed amount, his destitute loved ones might not have been able to afford a marker out of the pitifully small payment they likely received.

# THE ENGINE OF DEATH

The weather in New Albany can transform almost hourly. The weather on October 24, 1875, was a prime example. The days preceding that fall day had been cold and rainy, but on that Monday, an Indian summer warmed the citizens of New Albany. The sweet scent of the multitude of wildflowers growing in and around New Albany drifted throughout the city, the fragrance so pleasing that lovely afternoon that Josiah Gwin, editor of the *New Albany Daily Ledger*, wrote in his paper, "The gentle breezes wafted to our shores perfumes as delicious as those that swept over Araby the Blest," the reference from a silly little poem by Laura Elizabeth Richards popular at the time.

Philip Monney took a break from his labors to look up into the bright blue skies above New Albany. He breathed deeply of the sweet-scented air and then returned to his task. He liked his new job, and the hardworking thirty-one-year-old didn't want to disappoint his boss.

Monney, an immigrant from Switzerland, had recently moved with his wife, the former Sarah Ham, a twenty-two year-old native of the Hoosier State, and the couple's three daughters, seven-year-old Fannie, three-year-old Priscilla and two-year-old Hattie, to the city from nearby Salem, Indiana. He promptly found employment in the bustling little town, and the family settled into their new home near East Third Street. Sociable and friendly by nature, he and his equally outgoing wife quickly made friends with their neighbors. His girls seemed content in their new environs, and with his family happy, surrounded by new friends and with a job he truly enjoyed, Philip Monney was undoubtedly a happy man that beautiful fall day.

He couldn't have had even the slightest inkling of the calamity about to visit his family, a tragedy that would destroy his happy home and rip apart his loving family.

A little before one o'clock that afternoon, after her daughters Priscilla and Hattie finished lunch, Sarah, with her two young ones in tow, headed out to do some shopping for supper that evening. Hattie became cranky, and Sarah picked up her youngest daughter and carried her, holding the fidgety two-year-old in her arms as she led Priscilla by the hand along the tracks of the Short Line on Third Street. The one o'clock train approached the street and slowed to let off some passengers and allow others aboard the brightly colored intercity trolley. When Sarah stopped for the train, Hattie began squirming, and as she turned her attention to the wiggling bundle in her arms, Priscilla let go of her hand and dashed into the path of the oncoming train before anyone could stop her.

The train knocked the little girl down and under the front of the train. Though moving slowly to a stop, the car still had just enough forward momentum that the steel wheel made one revolution across Priscilla's tiny legs before coming to a complete halt. The merciless wheel severed one leg close to the thigh and crushed the other.

Onlookers carried her mangled body to the family's home. Summoned from his job, Philip quickly returned to the house. Told that nothing could be done to save the girl's life, the grieving father did his best to console his wife and comfort his dying daughter. After two hours of terrible suffering, little Priscilla died about three o'clock on that bright, sunny October day.

The family held her funeral the next day in the residence, a home so recently overflowing with laughter and love but now filled with the weeping and wails of the distraught family and their friends. Her loved ones laid Priscilla to rest in the Fairview Cemetery in the county plot near the burial ground's Main Avenue.

An inquest held that dreadful afternoon returned a verdict of accidental death, totally unavoidable by the company or its employees on the train. Though the verdict didn't blame Sarah, at least not officially, the town's tittle-tattlers quickly spread their opinions. The gossips claimed that Sarah should have paid more attention to her child, that she should have held more tightly to her daughter's tiny hand. "What kind of a mother is she?" they asked.

The wicked lecturers could have saved their breaths. Sarah blamed herself for her child's horrible suffering and death. Though Philip did his best to console his distressed spouse, she remained inconsolable. The stress produced by the horrible accident proved too much for the couple, and not long after, they divorced.

Philip went to Elizabeth, Indiana, and moved in with his parents, Martin and Frances Monney. He stayed in the town for the remainder of his life.

Sarah married Peter Russell on a June day in 1886. Still haunted by the death of her child, Sarah couldn't give her new husband the life he desired, and the couple divorced less than two years after the ceremony. She remained in New Albany and never remarried. Sarah most likely carried the responsibility of that tragic October day with her to her grave when she died in 1907.

# DEATH OF THE DINKY MAN

Sixty-eight-year-old John M. Williamson had a lifelong fascination with trains. He'd often sit in his backyard when off duty and watch them as they rolled along the tracks less than fifty yards from the backdoor of his two-story home at 1406 Dewey Street in the east end of New Albany. He'd bought the moderately sized house when he'd first moved to the city. His attraction to trains had shaped his career choice as a young man, and by the afternoon of Wednesday, January 19, 1916, he was credited with being the oldest conductor both in age and years of service to the Pennsylvania Railway Company, where he'd worked for the past forty-seven years.

He'd started working with the railroad as a passenger conductor on the Louisville and Indianapolis division of the company. Possessed of a genial disposition, he loved working with and meeting new people, and the position seemed the perfect one for him. He also had a strong work ethic, and this trait, when combined with his outgoing nature and passion for trains, meant he seldom missed a day's work. His supervisors noticed the hardworking conductor, and when a spot opened in the company's yard in Columbus, Indiana, they offered him the post.

The job paid more than he had earned as a conductor, and though he loved working with the passengers on his train and would miss them and his position, his growing family depended on him, and he quickly accepted the offer. His hard work and dedication quickly carried him up the company ladder, and before too long, the railroad promoted him to yardmaster. He worked just as hard in his new position for several years, but the high pressure and stress of the job took their toll. The long hours required of the position kept him away from his family more than he liked, and at the age of fifty, he was ready for a change.

John enjoyed watching steamboats as much as he enjoyed his trains, and when a position came open in 1898 as a conductor on the Dinky Line, an interurban track that ran between Louisville, Kentucky and New Albany, he immediately applied for the job. New Albany is located on the northern banks of the Ohio River, and steamboats and pleasure craft plied the sluggish stream. John could watch them for hours, but even when no boats passed up and down the mighty river, he liked to simply sit back and watch the sun's beams dance and play across the peaceful, sparkling waters.

# The Steel Wheels of Death

His outstanding record with the company worked in his favor. Though reluctant to lose the dedicated employee and the effort he put forth in making the Columbus yard efficient, the railroad granted his request, and John and his family moved south to the river city, buying their house on Dewey, just a little over a quarter mile from the waters of the mighty Ohio. By that chilly January day, he'd worked as a conductor on the line for almost eighteen years. Liked and admired by people in both Louisville and New Albany, his gregarious nature had made him many friends among the passengers who rode what he considered to be *his* train.

His missed his five children—three boys and two girls—now grown and raising their own families in other cities. One daughter, Mrs. Louis Wasch, lived far away in Salt Lake City, Utah, and the other one, Mrs. Emmons Ewing, lived in North Vernon, Indiana. Two of his sons, Percy and Charles, still lived in Columbus, and only one, John Jr., lived in New Albany. The distance meant that the family seldom gathered together, and he missed them dearly. Now that he and his wife lived alone in the house, the home that had once echoed with the sounds of children's laughter and play seemed so big and empty. However, his wife loved him, and he loved her in return, and that helped fill the vacant spaces. His many friends often stopped to visit, and all in all, John Williamson was a happy and contented fellow that sunny winter's day.

He was off work that Wednesday, and a little after ten o'clock that morning, he let his wife know that he was going down to watch the river for a bit. He told her he'd be back in time for lunch and then walked out the back door, through the yard and crossed the tracks of the New Albany Belt Line behind his home. He walked the short distance to the river and spent a little over an hour and a half walking west along the banks, dividing his attention between watching the river traffic moving up and down the stream and searching the banks for whatever the river had left behind.

Hungry and ready for his noon meal, he decided to head back home a little before noon. Instead of walking back along the riverbank, he turned north from the river and walked the short distance up to the railroad. When he reached the roadway, he turned east and slowly meandered along the tracks, looking to see what might have fallen from a passing train. He'd gotten to the crossing on East Fourteenth Street, less than a block from his home, when an eastbound Southern Railroad freight train passed him as he walked along the north side of the tracks. The train was a long one with one engine pulling from the front of the string of freight cars and one pushing from behind. Engineer Wallace Rocksby controlled the front engine, and engineer E.J. Pierce ran the rear engine. Conductor Joseph Hicks commanded the whole affair.

As the train crossed the street, Nicholas Bettinger, owner of a coal yard located near the crossing, looked out his office window at the passing train. Bettinger enjoyed watching the trains. He'd note the different styles of cars as they passed, and the assortment of things they carried always spiked his curiosity. When closed boxcars rolled along the tracks, he imagined all sorts of possible items contained within the wooden walls. He enjoyed the short break his observations afforded him from his duties, but that day, his pleasure turned to horror as he watched the sixteenth car in the long line strike his friend, John Williamson, and knock him under the passing cars.

The wheels of the car passed almost immediately over Williamson's head, mashing it to a pulp and mercifully giving him an almost instant death. Bettinger retched and tried to turn away from the appalling scene but couldn't. He watched in shock as the train continued to mangle Williamson's body. He finally gathered his wits about him, ran from his office and flagged down the train. Though Engineer Rocksby, unaware that his train had struck anyone, wondered why the man yelled for him to stop, he quickly applied the brakes, slowly bringing the behemoth to a stop. Bettinger horrified Rocksby when the coalman told the engineer that his train had just killed Williamson. None of the other workmen on the train knew anything of the incident, either.

Floyd County coroner Dr. C.E. Briscoe, summoned to the scene, examined Williamson's battered remains. He determined that Williamson had been walking too close to the train when the car struck him, and in his opinion the railroad bore no responsibility for the accident. When Briscoe finished his observation, workers from Lottick Brother's Undertakers hauled the badly mangled corpse to the brother's business on the corner of East Fourth and Spring Streets and prepared the remains for burial. As talented as they may have been at their chosen profession, there isn't much even today's morticians, with all of their advanced techniques and technology, can do to restore a head reduced to pulp to a condition that would make the dead one presentable, and once the undertakers had finished their gruesome task, they took Williamson's closed casket to his home. A funeral was hastily held that same afternoon before the decomposing body started to release any offensive odors.

John M. Williamson, devoted husband, father and friend, industrious and outgoing, had spent his entire life dedicated to working around the trains he so loved. How unfortunate that death would come to him under the grinding steel wheels of one.

## CUT TO PIECES

Anna Trunk couldn't sleep. The throbbing pain in her tooth seemed to radiate through her entire head with every beat of her heart as she tossed and turned in her bed that Easter night in 1886. She desperately needed to get some sleep. Her husband, Henry, a popular paper hanger in New Albany, had to work the next morning, and she'd have to tend to her two sick children without his help.

Her devoted husband had tenderly cared for the children, Cleo and Gilbert, both of whom had been suffering from the whooping cough for the past several days, as well as seeing to his wife's needs over the holiday weekend, but Anna knew she needed to get some rest before he left if she was going to have the strength to care for them. Though she hated to do so, she finally woke Henry about three thirty and asked if he could go get some pain medication to help ease her suffering enough so that she could catch a little bit of sleep in the few remaining hours left to her that torturous night.

Henry knew her request meant he wouldn't get anymore sleep before he had to be at work, but he loved his wife deeply, an affection equally returned, and rose without a complaint from the couple's warm bed. Dressed against the chilly night air, he grabbed a metal bucket to get some water while he was out and then walked out of the family's home on East Spring Street a little before four o'clock that morning. He headed west on the wide, tree-lined avenue and bought the pain reliever his wife had requested, as well as some medication for his children, in the drugstore on the northwest corner of East Spring and East Fifteenth Streets just a short distance from his house. He filled his pail with water, and as he stood on the west side of East Fifteenth patiently waiting for the slow-moving freight train making its way south along the tracks of the Louisville, New Albany & Chicago Railroad running down the center of the street, he decided to head for a butcher shop on Market Street in order to get some breakfast meat. He planned on having the meal ready for his family before waking them and leaving for work. Thinking a ride would be faster than walking, he prepared to jump aboard one of the slow-moving cars.

A little after five o'clock that spring morning, two unnamed men, walking south on the tracks from Spring Street, noticed something lying to one side of the tracks. In the darkness, they couldn't identify the object lying in the unlit street, but as they got closer, they noticed another pile a few feet south of the first mysterious item. Interested to see what might have fallen from a passing train, they hurried their pace and were horrified to discover the lower torso and badly bruised and cut legs of a man. As they ran to the next pile, they noticed the stringy intestines and other innards strung out along the tracks before finding the rest of Henry, his arms equally bruised and deeply cut. The stunned duo immediately notified the authorities.

Henry had apparently lost his footing when he'd attempted to board the car. Perhaps the pail of water had thrown off his balance, or maybe the water itself had caused him to slip. Whatever the reason for the fall, at least death had come fairly instantaneously for twenty-nine-year-old Henry Trunk. His remains were gathered together and "put in shape for burial." Floyd County coroner Dr. J.H. Lemon ruled the death accidental.

A large number of his friends attended the funeral, held in the family residence that afternoon. Henry rests in Plat 10, Range 13, Lot 4, Grave 1, in the Fairview Cemetery. Anna, just shy of her twenty-fourth birthday when her husband died, never remarried. When she died in Louisville on June 22, 1948, exactly one month after her eighty-sixth birthday, her body was returned to New Albany and buried next to her beloved Henry.

# Part III
# Suicides

*There is a division of opinion whether it requires a coward or a brave man to end his earthly existence by his own hand. The question may be discussed, pro and con, for all time to come, yet, occasionally a human being runs the risk of whether suicide is right or wrong, and deliberately dies by his own act.*
—*Josiah Gwin, editor of the* New Albany Public Press, *June 3, 1885.*

The Grim Reaper seldom announces ahead of time when he will visit us to collect his harvest of souls, and the unfortunate individuals thus far mentioned had little or no warning of their impending date with destiny. The ones that did have some small notice most likely fought against their demise with all the strength they could muster; self-preservation is one of, if not *the*, strongest motivations of even the simplest of living organisms, from single-celled amoeba to us humans. Even the remotest possibility of death is generally avoided at all costs.

There are, of course, exceptions to this rule. Parents voluntarily and without thought of self, run into burning houses in the attempt to save their children. Lovers willingly sacrifice their individual lives to protect their loved ones. Soldiers selflessly throw themselves on live grenades in an attempt to save the lives of their comrades, allowing their bodies to absorb the force of the devastating blast and death-dealing shrapnel.

Japanese kamikaze pilots opted for early deaths in defense of their emperor. On February 18, 2010, Andrew Joseph Strack III, a computer engineer with marital troubles and angry with the United States Internal Revenue Service, emulated these pilots when he flew his single-engine, fixed-wing Piper PA-28-236 into the offices of the IRS in Austin, Texas, killing himself and sixty-eight-year-old Vernon Hunter. Hunter, a government employee and twenty-year veteran of the United States Army, had survived two tours in Vietnam, but Strack's crazed desire for revenge made Hunter's wife a widow and robbed the veteran's three children, three stepchildren, seven grandchildren and one great-grandchild of their father and grandparent.

However, on occasion, some people, like Strack, eagerly look forward to their own demise, and many often commit whatever actions they believe will hasten the end of their lives. These acts are commonly called suicide. According to the National Institute of Mental Health, suicide was the eleventh leading cause of death in the United States in 2006, accounting for approximately 33,000 fatalities. This means that self-destruction caused approximately 11 out of every 100,000 American deaths that year. More than twice as many Americans killed themselves that year than were murdered by other Americans.

For every successful suicide, another approximately twelve to twenty-five attempted suicides are made. Men are four times more likely to succeed in killing themselves than women, and in 2006, suicide was the seventh leading cause of death for men versus the sixteenth leading cause for women. Though men over the age of fifty are the most likely to end their own lives, children as young as ten who commit suicide account for almost 2 out of every 100,000 deaths of children between ten and fourteen years of age. Again, young boys and men are four times more likely to end their own lives than are their female counterparts, and while adolescent boys and young men are more likely to use firearms to achieve their sought-after release, for children ten and younger, suffocation is the preferred method of suicide.

Firearms are the preferred method for most people of all ages who choose self-destruction, followed by suffocation and poison, but the ways in which people choose to end their own lives are as varied as the motivations behind these unnatural deaths. Some jump in front of moving automobiles. Others leap from tall buildings, and every now and then, some slit their own throats.

The motivations behind these actions have always amazed me. In some cases, the reason why someone chose to end his or her life will be quite clear, but in others, we may never know why the individual picked such a gruesome ending, and though suicide is the official cause given for some deaths, other, more sinister reasons may actually have caused the early departures.

## "I Dread the Night in This Gloomy Building"

Thirty-nine-year-old Enoch West spent the early part of Tuesday evening, November 3, 1885, methodically sharpening his pocketknife in front of the tea store where he worked at what was then 46 Market Street in downtown New Albany. Though his employer, James H. Forman, considered him an "exceptionally faithful, quiet and industrious clerk," West didn't earn enough money for a proper home, and so he slept on the second floor of the building on a dingy pallet covered with old quilts and empty coffee sacks. He'd both lived and worked there for the past decade.

Despite his pitiful economic station and generally melancholy nature, those who knew West liked him, and the quiet and highly respected young man was a member in good standing of both the local chapter of the International Order of Odd Fellows and the Jefferson Lodge of Free Masons in New Albany.

Passersby noticed how meticulously he stroked the burnished blade across the oiled stone. He'd slowly and steadily pull the blade toward him, then, flipping the shiny steel over, he'd push the blade away from him with an equally firm and sturdy stroke, honing the cutting edge of the knife until razor sharp. He'd stop periodically and slowly pull the blade across his thumbnail, testing the sharpness of the steel edge.

A female acquaintance stopped to talk with him at a little past nine o'clock, and when asked how he felt that chilly evening, the downhearted clerk replied, "I've never felt so blue in my life." His lady friend told him perhaps he should go to bed—a good night's sleep might improve his demeanor by the morning—but he just shrugged his shoulders and said, "I dread the night in this gloomy building, and I rarely sleep when I retire." The pair made idle chitchat for a few more minutes, and when his female companion left, Enoch folded the blade back into the body of the knife, put the tool in his pocket and then spent the next hour or so aimlessly wandering the downtown area.

When he returned, he went inside and stoked the fire in the wood stove, and the last anyone saw of him that cool fall night, Enoch West sat by the stove in the dimly lit store, his face buried in his hands as he wrestled with the demons running wild in his mind.

Only West knows for certain what horrible thoughts tormented him that frosty night as he sat alone in the foreboding darkness. Perhaps he thought about his father, who died insane, or maybe he thought of his brother, an "incurable lunatic" held in the Floyd County asylum. Enoch lived in fear that he might one day go insane because he knew the little money he earned would provide little or no treatment options that would save him from the living death of madness.

By all accounts, he was a hardworking and conscientious man, despite his constant despair, and so Forman was surprised when he arrived at the business about 7:30 a.m. the next morning only to find that his usually prompt clerk hadn't already opened the store. Forman rattled and beat on the door. He called repeatedly for West but received no reply. Assuming his employee had either overslept or was sick, Forman unhurriedly strolled next door to the dry goods store of Mr. James Peake. He asked if Peake knew why West hadn't opened the store and didn't answer his repeated calls to come and open the door. Peake said he hadn't the foggiest notion and offered to enter the building through a door in the back.

Peake entered the store and made his way to the second floor, where Enoch usually slept. After searching the floor and finding no sign of the missing man, Peake walked up the stairs to the building's third and final floor. Almost as soon as he reached the landing, he found the missing clerk… dead as a doornail and covered in blood.

At some point during the previous night, Enoch's dark thoughts finally convinced him that he had only one sure escape from the insanity he feared. Once he arrived at his decision, he carried his pallet, quilts and empty coffee sacks up to the third floor. He arranged his bundle amidst the dust and debris and then gazed through the window for a last look at Market Street. When finished, he lay on his bed, composed himself for the task to which he'd set his mind and, once comfortably situated, took the knife from his pocket and opened the razor-sharp blade. Holding the knife in his left hand, West cut his throat from just under his left ear to his windpipe. Almost unbelievably, he then switched the weapon to his right hand and inflicted an even more frightful cut, cutting completely across his throat from ear to ear and slicing open the arteries on both sides of his neck. He then folded his arms over his forehead, crossed his feet and probably died within five minutes. Nothing indicated that he'd struggled after his deadly act, and when found, Enoch still tightly grasped the knife in his right hand.

Peake ran as fast as he could down the three flights of stairs and, in a voice choked with fear and horror, breathlessly informed Forman of his gruesome discovery. Forman called for William Merker, a local undertaker, and summoned acting Coroner Starr. Starr determined that Enoch West had committed suicide, "while under mental aberration," and no foul play was suspected.

His brother Odd Fellows, who had charge of his funeral, carried Enoch West, the innocent victim of insanity in one way or another for most of his life, to his grave in the Fairview Cemetery that Friday, November 6, 1885. According to the editor of the *New Albany Daily Ledger*, his lodge brothers "should, and doubtless will…drop sympathetic tears upon his grave."

# "A Very Unpleasant and Painful Act"

Sometime toward the middle of May 1885, sixty-five-year-old Thomas G. Gorman arrived in New Albany. History doesn't note how Mr. Gorman made his way to the city. He may have come by train, or he may have leisurely traveled here by one of the numerous steamboats that regularly stopped along New Albany's riverfront. He could have come by stagecoach or on horseback, but Thomas Gorman was a desperate man, and considering his financial situation at the time, he may have simply walked to the city from his home.

After his marriage to Lydia Moore in Springfield, Illinois, on January 11, 1876, he and his new bride enjoyed a comfortable existence in their modest home on the northeast corner of Thirteenth and Washington Streets in that city. Thomas, by all accounts a sober, reliable worker, supported the couple as a carpenter. He quit his carpentry career when he landed a much-sought-after position with the Louisville, New Albany & Chicago Railroad

Company, the LNA&C, as an engineer and master mechanic, a position he held for several years.

When not at work, he enjoyed spending the fourth Monday of every month with his fellow Masons in the Central Lodge #71 and the first Thursday of most months enjoying the companionship of his fellow Masons in the Ellwood Commandery #6. Ironically, this fellowship may have led to his downfall.

The Masons are a respectable group of Christian men, and we can reasonably expect that they allowed no alcohol consumption during the meetings (though only a Mason knows what takes place within the walls of the Masonic Temple during the secretive gatherings). However, most men drink when they gather in a group, and while alcohol may have been forbidden during the meetings, the men could have easily retired to a local saloon after the event. Somehow, somewhere, Thomas Gorman became a drunk, and his intemperate habits eventually cost him his coveted position with the railroad.

Unable to find work and in danger of losing his home, Thomas quit drinking and soon found other work. Unfortunately, he wasn't able to maintain his sobriety, and when unknown "trouble from other quarters" knocked him "off balance," he went on a "tare [sic]," which nearly ruined him with his friends. His drunken rampage is also probably why his beloved Lydia left him about this time.

Determined to right the wrongs he'd done, he quit drinking and set about making amends to those he'd offended. He left Springfield and made his way to New Albany, at the time Indiana's largest city. Though the area's economy was slowly falling into a recession, the busy river town was still a likely place to find a good-paying job. Thomas, with a limited amount of funds, rented a room for one dollar a day in the Central Hotel, located on the southwest corner of Market and Bank Streets in downtown New Albany.

Optimistic he'd quickly find work, he began his job search almost immediately, but despite his best efforts to secure a position, finding work in a strange city without anyone to recommend him proved difficult. His inability to land a spot soon depressed the once hopeful senior citizen. He resumed his former bad habits and soon spent what little money he had left on drinking.

By Monday afternoon, May 25, 1885, Thomas had run through his small bankroll. With no money left to buy his supper, pay for his hotel bill or find what solace he could get from the bottle, Thomas Gorman decided he'd reached the end of his rope. The desperate man wrote a letter to the proprietor of the Central Hotel, Mr. Francis M. Tribbey. The letter read:

*Central Hotel, New Albany, May 25.—F.M. Tribbey, Esq. Proprietor—*

*Dear Sir:*

*I have a very unpleasant and painful act to perform, perhaps this afternoon. It is no less than to die by my own hand. As there will be many inquiries as to the why and the wherefore, I will not say much, as I am too nervous to write. I have for a few years past been unfortunate in many ways, and lost in one way all my property, besides a good position as Master Mechanic. That set me back for a while and I felt badly, but I recovered from it, and have held other and better places since, and could have kept them, too, if I had not allowed trouble from other quarters to get me off my balance, and I went on a "tare" for a few days, which nearly ruined me with my friends, as I was all my life known as a sober man.*

*I had difficulty to recover and get a job again, which I did after a while. I did not take any more drink, nor do I while engaged in business. But I am at the present time out of a job, out of money, out of home, wife, or friends, in a strange city. I ought to die and get out of the way. J.B. Carson, W.R. Woodard and J.C. McDoel, of the L.N.A. & C. railroad, know me well. Mr. Bettis master mechanic, not so well.*

*I am also a free and accepted Mason, of Central Lodge No. 71, Springfield, Ill., of Springfield Chapter No. 1 (or 7) and of Ellwood Commandery No. 6 K.T. I would like to be buried as a mason:*

*I am sorry I could not pay you all I owe; but what few things that are in my valise are not worth much, but my watch, if you wish to keep it, is good. But I know that the expense will be greater than all their value. You will no doubt say, Why did he come to New Albany? I came here in the hope of getting a place, but was disappointed. My wife was at Chalmer's Station, Ind., the last I heard from her. I have not seen her for about twenty months. I will leave a letter to be forwarded if I die, to Chalmers or Logansport. I would be thankful to you if you would have Mr. Bettis notified. He will notify Chicago friends. I am not particular where I am buried, so I get a decent burial. I have also a sister, Susan Costello, at Dayton, O.*

*I am in my sober senses, and do not like to die; but "I put my trust in God" and believe "my faith is well founded." I hope He will forgive me, and I also hope you will. Good bye. Brother, pray for me a sinner, and forgive me. Yours in fraternity.*
T.G. GORMAN

Apparently, either Gorman couldn't bring himself to end his life that afternoon or he lacked the means to do so. While we will likely never know why he didn't end his life that day, we do know that two days later, dressed in his best clothes, he sat down in a high-backed chair against the wall in a corner of his room; stretched his legs out in front of him, crossing the left over the right; crossed his left arm over his chest; and, with his right hand, placed a Smith & Wesson .22-caliber pistol up against his right temple and pulled the trigger.

No one heard the gunshot. Approximately two hours later, the desk clerk came to investigate why Gorman hadn't appeared to settle his bill for room and board and discovered the body. Gorman's head lay back against the wall, his face and neck covered in blood, which still oozed from the wound in the side of his head. His body was warm.

On a table beside him lay the letter he'd written to Tribby, along with several others addressed to various former friends and loved ones, including Lydia. On the sheet upon which he'd written to the hotel's proprietor two days before, Gorman had added the following:

*New Albany, May 27.—I was until to-day in hope, but I am in despair this A.M. If there are any newspaper remarks send one to my wife, one to my sister, in Dayton, O., and one to Dr. Rutledge, No. 1,410 Olive street St. Louis. Thanking you very much and regretting the trouble and expense I am to you, I will get ready to leave, as I see no other way to avoid it: and I am ashamed to meet you. Do not think I am insane. I have had trouble enough to make me so, but I am not. I am about to die and will make no charges against any one. Please send my private papers to my wife. Farewell, brother. T.G. Gorman*

The Masonic Lodge in New Albany saw that Thomas Gorman received a decent burial. His remains rest in Plot 10, Range 6, Lot 37, in the Fairview

Cemetery. If a stone once marked his grave, nothing but grass covers the spot today. Only a handful of people knew of the life and death of Thomas Gorman—until now.

# Mrs. Manor's Self-Murder

Louisa A. Curry, daughter of Doctor Thompson Curry and his wife, Mahala, took her first breath in February 1854 in Floyd County, Indiana. About six months after her twentieth birthday, on October 28, 1874, she married William A. Manor, a Civil War veteran of Company D of the 186th Ohio Volunteer Infantry. The young couple desperately wanted a child to add to their happy household, but more than ten years passed before they joyfully welcomed the arrival of their first child, a son they named after his father, in 1884. After trying unsuccessfully for so many heartbreaking years, the couple was ecstatic. They doted on their young son and provided him with all the love and attention they could muster.

Unfortunately, young William passed away when he was only eight months old. He died of "cholera infantum" on Tuesday evening, July 21, 1885, the death sending his mother on a slow descent into madness. She spent hours weeping over the grave of her beloved child, and William often had to drag her away from the site. She refused to eat or take care of herself, and their once tidy home quickly deteriorated into a filthy hovel of unmade beds, unwashed dishes and general disorder.

William, a foreman in the DePauw Glass Works factory, did what he could to maintain the home and care for the woman he so adored, but his position at the glassworks required long hours at the factory away from his distraught wife. He grew so concerned about the mental state of his beloved that in October 1885, he sent her to live with his parents in Xenia, Ohio, believing they could give her the attention and care he couldn't provide her.

Shortly after her arrival, Louisa disappeared. Family and friends searched for the missing woman and finally found her standing half-nude in a pond on the property. She'd attempted to drown herself, but the shallow, chilly waters prevented her from attaining the reunion with her son she so desperately sought. William's father waded into the waist-deep water and brought a fighting Louisa to the shore. Wrapped in a blanket to preserve her modesty and ward off the effects of the cold water, she was carried to the house and locked in a bedroom on the second floor of the home.

Two days after the incident in the pond, someone unbelievably and quite carelessly left the door to her second-floor bedroom unlocked. Discovering the unsecured door, Louisa wasted no time in making her second attempt at escaping the misery that was her life since the death of her darling child. She made a mad dash down the long hallway and dove through a window at the end of the corridor. Fortunately (or unfortunately, depending on who's point of view), Louisa's attempt only succeeded in breaking her arm, which added more pain and suffering to her already pitiful existence.

Less than a week later, when a family servant brought lunch to her room, Louisa made her move. When the young girl opened the door to Louisa's room, the distraught mother pushed past her and ran down the hallway again. This time, she dove headfirst through the just-repaired window, and one wonders if her first attempt had taught her the importance of going headfirst when jumping from such a low height. To the shock and horror of those watching, she dashed her brains out on the concrete sidewalk below the window, creating a gory mess that some unfortunate soul had to cleanup. The family had her remains brought back to New Albany, where they buried her in the Fairview Cemetery.

William eventually put this terrible tragedy behind him and married Pickaway County, Ohio native Harriet J. Hammond less than two years later, on September 3, 1887, in Delaware County, Indiana. The new Mrs. Manor, thirty-six when she and William were married, later bore her husband a daughter they named Jennie Louise. Harriet died less than twenty years later, in 1905, at the ripe old age of fifty-four. William apparently had had enough of so-called "married bliss." He didn't remarry and passed away thirteen years later, in 1918, at the age of seventy-two. He is buried next to Louisa, who lies between her husband and her son. I don't know where Harriet's remains repose in their eternal slumber.

Louisa's death is an excellent example of how a relatively innocuous item can alter history. Though this change to the reality of our history is minor, I think this incident at least shows that the potential for a screw-up with major impact exists.

I don't know who reported Louisa's death, but that person's obvious speech impediment has altered Louisa's legacy for more than one hundred years; at least, I assume a speech impediment caused her obituary to call her "Weda." The cemetery records of the Fairview Cemetery also list "Weda" Manor as buried in the plot where Louisa lies between her two loves.

# A Horrible Sight

Thirty-eight-year-old Gustave Schmadel, a "sober and industrious" immigrant to America, made his living in Gotham, New York, as a baker in the city's finest hotels. Those who knew him described him as a kind and indulgent father and a devoted husband. His family was equally devoted to their hardworking parent and spouse. Though he worked long hours in less than pleasant conditions, he enjoyed his work, which enabled him and his family to enjoy a moderate lifestyle. But years spent in the dusty conditions of the bakeries where he worked caused him to develop respiratory problems. The filthy air in the city only compounded his health issues, and he determined to find a town where the air was cleaner, the people friendlier and the pace of life a bit slower.

In 1889, leaving his loving family behind, he set out in search of such a place. History leaves us no account of how long he searched or by what means he traveled, but we do know that in the winter of that year, he came to New Albany to visit cousins living there. After spending some time in the city, "he was so pleased with the country and the great improvement to his health" that he returned to New York, gathered his wife, his six-year-old son and eight-year-old daughter, packed their belongings and the happy little quartet made their way back to the town, arriving in New Albany sometime in March 1890. He rented a house at what was then 383 Upper Elm Street, and not long afterward, purchased the meat store of Charles Krementz on the corner of East Eighth and Sycamore[8] Streets, where he began preparations to open a meat shop and produce store. His pleasant personality and diligent work ethic quickly made him several friends, and his health rapidly improved in the area's clean air. Schmadel surely considered himself a lucky man.

Unfortunately, a few weeks after his arrival, as he went about the business of preparing his planned shop, he suffered a relapse of his respiratory condition, which led to his confinement to his bed for several weeks. Unable to continue his work, Jacob became "gloomy and morose." By the night of Wednesday, April 30, though able to get out of bed and move about his once happy house, his condition had worsened. The normally stoic baker complained constantly that day about the pains in his chest. He finally surrendered to the pain and retired early that evening in a "terrible state of depression."

His wife woke when Jacob rose from the bed at about three thirty the next morning and walked into an adjoining room. Thinking he had gone for a drink of water, she stayed in the bed, drifting in and out of sleep, for about another hour. Noticing that her husband hadn't returned, she became concerned that "a sudden spell of sickness had seized him" and rose from her bed in search of him. She searched through the house but found no sign of her beloved spouse. Her apprehension growing by the minute, she went out into the yard and continued her exploration. When she didn't locate him outside, the worried woman returned to the house, and that's when she noticed the open cellar door.

Peering down the stairs into the ominous darkness, she saw a figure lying prostrate on the basement floor. Fearing her husband had either fallen down the stairs or had suffered a seizure, she quickly descended the steps. Reaching the bottom, she raised her lamp and found Jacob. Holding the light over his prostrate form, she bent down and was shocked to see a huge, gaping wound in his throat. His blood, still oozing from the wound when his wife found him, stained "his night clothes a crimson dye." A bloody razor lay near his body, and the realization quickly dawned on her that her darling Jacob had committed suicide. Her "heart-rending screams" woke her children and her neighbors, and they came to her assistance.

The neighbors carried Jacob's still warm body upstairs, while others tried to comfort the distraught family. Floyd County coroner W.L. Starr came to the house and examined the body. He found that Jacob had committed suicide by literally cutting his throat from ear to ear with the sharp razor, severing both carotid arteries and his windpipe. Before slashing his throat, he'd also cut open the artery in his left arm near the hand.

Jacob Schmadel left no suicide note to explain his actions, but many believed the return of his illness drove him to commit the act. The following night, Thursday, May 2, the family returned his body to New York via the Ohio & Mississippi Railroad and buried their loved one near the city. Not long after, his widow sold the home and business, and she and the children returned to New York.

They'd arrived in New Albany happy and optimistic about their prospects in their new city, but in just a little over six weeks, they left the town in the deepest misery they'd ever known, their once bright future now bleak and uncertain. I have no idea what became of the family.

# If Only He Hadn't Kicked the Bucket

John Schueler worked in his father's butcher shop for most of his life. Charles Schueler had a reputation as an honest man. His shop sold quality meat at reasonable prices, and the business had a large clientele. Though John's wages provided his family with a moderate lifestyle, when he heard of Frederick Saam's plan to sell his business, a profitable meat market and green grocery located on the corner of East Eighth Street and Culbertson Avenue near the Fairview Cemetery, Schueler decided to strike out on his own. Sometime during the winter of 1900–01, the optimistic New Albanian purchased Saam's building and business, moved his family into Saam's former quarters on the top floor and continued the grocery and meat business on the lower one.

He'd gambled everything on his venture, but the business didn't turn out to be as prosperous as Schueler hoped. The cheerful and attentive grocer slowly sunk into a deep depression. He became absent-minded and acted strange. Alarmed at the changes in his behavior, his customers started taking their trade elsewhere, causing the business to slide further downhill. As his commerce dwindled away to almost nothing, Schueler slipped deeper and deeper into the gloom clouding his thoughts, his slow descent into madness culminating in one final act of insanity in the predawn hours of an early spring day.

Schueler kept a horse in a stable behind his business/home. He usually rose early in the morning to tend to the animal, and his wife thought nothing of it when he left their bed a little after four o'clock on the morning on Sunday, March 31, 1901. His wife, like so many of us who enjoy those last sweet moments lingering in bed before duty drives us from our comfy nest, didn't get up when her husband did, and she watched her husband dress from under the warm blankets. Before he left the chilly room, she noticed him take some money from one of his pants pockets and place the currency on the mantle of the fireplace. She lazed in her peaceful sanctuary, enjoying the silence for a few more minutes, then rose and dressed.

Mrs. Schueler went to her kitchen and prepared breakfast for her husband and four children. Her two boys and two girls still slept, and when she finished the meal, she briefly considered waking them before calling to her husband but decided that, since it was a Sunday, she'd let them sleep just a bit longer and instead called out the back door for John. She turned back to her tasks, setting the food on the table along with the plates and eating utensils, and forgot about her husband until she'd finished her preparations. She wondered why he hadn't come in yet and thought perhaps he hadn't heard her call. Not wanting to wake her neighbors with a louder summons, she bundled up against the chilly morning air and walked out to the stable to let him know his breakfast waited.

She crossed the short distance from her back door to the stable, opened the door…and in the sputtering lamplight saw her husband's lifeless corpse slowly swinging from a halter strap attached to a rafter in the building, his feet barely clearing the dirt floor as his body leisurely swayed back and forth in the flickering light.

Her agonized screams woke the neighbors she'd been so concerned about just moments before, and they came rushing to her aid. They carried the grief-stricken widow back to the house and then summoned the Floyd County coroner, Dr. William L. Starr. The physician first examined the hanging corpse and then made an investigation of the small stable. When finished with his exploration, Starr determined that Schueler's death had been an unwavering effort by the depressed grocer to end his life and not an accident or murder. Only then did the coroner order the lifeless body cut down and taken to Kraft's undertakers.

The coroner determined that after tending to his horse, Schueler (either thirty-five or thirty-eight, depending on which obituary one believes) had taken one of the animal's halters, tied one end of the leather straps around his neck, upended a bucket and then stood on the pail as he tied the other end of the strap around the rafter. Only John knows how long he stood there before kicking the bucket away.

After a service in St. Mary's Catholic Church two days later, the distraught family buried his remains in the church's cemetery on Charlestown Road. He left no note explaining his final frantic act, but most everyone agreed that depression over his failing business is what prompted him to "kick the bucket."

## TRAGEDY ON THANKSGIVING DAY

McClellan Sinkhorn and his wife, Ruth, raised eight children in a tiny shotgun house on Ekin Avenue in the early years of the nineteenth century. He supported his rather large family as a piano tuner in New Albany, and though the quality of his work put him in great demand in the city, the work wasn't steady; his wages barely sustained his large brood. There wasn't much left to spend on entertainment, and in the days before radio or television, the family found joy in simple things, often spending their leisure time reading, talking or singing.

When the weather allowed, the brothers, like many young men in New Albany, loved to play baseball. The city has a fairly illustrious baseball history, and five native New Albanians—Noble Wayne LaMaster, David Bruce McDonald, John Peter "Jack" Heinzman, George Jouett Meekin and Billy Herman—all first played the game on one of the city's many diamonds before eventually playing professionally in the sport's Major Leagues.[9] Though they never achieved the status of these individuals, the five Sinkhorn brothers—William, Leslie, Harold, Merrill and Lloyd—all had an inherent talent for the game. Their father encouraged his sons, and the naturally athletic youngsters played where and when they could. The quintet became quite popular in the city due to their talents and abilities. As they grew older, all five played in the city's amateur leagues, and more than one opposing team simply forfeited the game when faced with all five brothers at once.

Baseball wasn't the only outdoor activity the boys enjoyed with their father. McClellan took his sons into the outdoors as often as possible. The boys liked the time spent with their father in the wilderness surrounding New Albany, and whether hunting, fishing or just admiring the beauty of nature, the experiences they shared with their father imparted in them a lifelong love of the great outdoors. That love would eventually result in tragedy, but by the time the terrible event occurred the boys had become accustom to heartbreak, especially the youngest son, Lloyd.

McClellan had a beautiful voice and loved to sing inspirational hymns. When not leading his family in singing the songs of praise, he led the choir of the Main Street Methodist Episcopal Church, and his reputation as one of the area's finest gospel singers quickly spread. Congregations across the state invited the talented singer to perform in their churches, and he accepted the offers as much as possible. He sang in five churches in the city of French Lick, Indiana, on Sunday, November 27, 1921, and the energy and enthusiasm he put into singing the praises of his God proved too much for the sixty-one-year-old. He developed pneumonia early the following week, and by Friday morning, his health had declined to the point that Reverend J.B. Starr, in whose house McClellan stayed during his visit, notified Ruth of her husband's rapidly deteriorating condition. Ruth left New Albany immediately but arrived in French Lick too late. Her husband was dead. The *New Albany Daily Ledger* noted his passing the next day: "The sweet and tender notes of the singer were stilled forever, and hushed were the story of the love and the kindness of the Creator in the mouth of the evangelist. Five days from the time his songs went out into the hearts of others, his own heart was stilled."

On Saturday morning, Ruth shipped his body via the Monon Railroad to New Albany. The remains arrived in the city that evening, and the undertakers of Seabrook & Peters prepared McClellan for burial. Reverend Howerton of the Main Street Methodist Church conducted the funeral in the family's tiny home at two thirty on Monday afternoon, and the family laid their patriarch to rest in the Fairview Cemetery.

The passing devastated the Sinkhorn clan, which was not in the best economic situation to start, both emotionally and financially. The older boys went to work to support the family, but Ruth insisted that her younger children stay in school. Time eventually healed the pain of their father's loss, and they went on with their lives.

In 1927, Lloyd, a handsome man about six feet, two inches tall with black hair and dark, flashing eyes, met Ruth Baggerly, a petite blond-haired, blue-eyed beauty from nearby Borden, Indiana, and the couple married in April of the following year. Lloyd got a good position in a veneer factory, fortunate to find the work in those early years of America's Great Depression. His wages allowed the couple to eventually buy a small home. Though diminutive, the house was bigger than the ones in which either had grown up, and the newlyweds, both from large families, anticipated raising a large brood of their own. Not long after they bought the home at 2145 East Elm Street, Ruth gave birth to their first child, a son they named Lloyd "Jack," in February 1932. Lloyd was a proud and doting father, and with the arrival of his son, he surely felt satisfied with his life. He threw himself into his family and his work, though he continued to play baseball and hunt and fish whenever he got the chance.

His happiness ended just two months later when his beloved mother died unexpectedly during the night of Wednesday, April 20. The fifty-eight-year-old passed away in her home at 1802 Beeler Street in New Albany. Though a member of the Depauw Memorial Methodist Church, her children held the funeral in her home at two thirty the following Friday afternoon and afterward buried her beside McClellan in the Fairview Cemetery.

Though grief-stricken at the loss of his darling mother, Lloyd had his own family now and soon recovered from his sorrow as he busied himself with his job, his love of nature, baseball and caring for his wife and son. He enjoyed a prosperous, peaceful life for the next six years, until his beloved Ruth suddenly became ill in the summer of 1938.

She suffered agonizing pain in her abdomen for several months, and unable to properly care for her husband and weary from the never-ending pain, she fell into a deep depression as summer turned to fall. Labor Day came and went, and then Halloween. Ruth's depression and hurt grew worse with each passing day. Lloyd's extended family and hers planned a get-together for Thanksgiving, and he hoped the reunion would brighten Ruth's spirits and take her mind off her pain, at least temporarily.

Heavy, wet snowflakes started falling in New Albany during the early morning hours of Thursday, November 24, 1938. The city's first snowfall continued after sunrise. When the flakes stopped falling a little before ten o'clock that morning, an inch and a half of snow blanketed the city, but by noon that Thanksgiving Day 1938, the skies had cleared, and the bright sunshine reflecting in the ice crystals created a dazzling display of dancing diamonds.

Lloyd probably paid little attention to the beautiful scene.

Sometime during the night, Ruth left her husband and six-year-old son in the couple's warm bed and walked into an adjoining room. She took her husband's .20-gauge shotgun, loaded the weapon and then sat alone in the dark room. Who knows what thoughts went through her head as she sat there in the shadows, the dreadful pain in her abdomen pushing her closer and closer to the edge of madness. Did she think of her husband, gently snoring in the other room? Did she wonder about little Lloyd? Perhaps she thought if she removed the offending part, her pain would cease, because shortly before seven thirty that snowy morning, when escape from the pain in her stomach became more important to her than either her husband or her son, Ruth placed the barrel against her stomach, bent over the piece and pulled the trigger.

Father and son both heard the shot. Lloyd immediately jumped from the bed, telling little Jack, "Stay in bed!" before rushing from the bedroom. He found Ruth lying in an in a rapidly growing pool of blood. Lloyd rushed to his unresponsive wife. Leaving her on the floor, he called for help. A police car soon arrived, and Little Jack, unaware of what had happened, watched through the frosty bedroom window as they loaded his mother in the folded-down backseat of the convertible cruiser and then drove away.

Still alive despite her terrible wound, Ruth was taken to St. Edwards Hospital. Both families gathered at the hospital on Spring Street that Thanksgiving Day 1938, praying and trying to console the almost inconsolable husband. Some of the more optimistic members believed that with every passing hour, Ruth's chances for survival grew stronger. A little before seven o'clock that night, one of his aunts took Jack in to see his mother. As he sat on her bed, she looked at him and said, "Jackie, I want you to be a good boy." These were words the last words she'd ever speak to her son.

At seven thirty in the evening, twelve hours after she'd sought relief from the pain tearing at her insides, Ruth Sinkhorn found the release she'd sought and eased gently into eternity. She left no note explaining her drastic actions to the grieving husband and motherless son she left behind.

Her body lay in state at the Seabrook funeral home at 1119 East Market Street on Friday, and a stream of visitors paid their last respects, doing their best to comfort the grief-stricken husband. Her funeral took place at two o'clock on Saturday, and Lloyd had her remains laid to rest in the Graceland Memorial Park on Charlestown Road.

Jackie spent time with different members of both his father's and mother's families, attending seven schools in his first six years. Though shuffled between homes as his father coped with the loss of his wife, Jackie's relatives all treated him good, accepting him into their immediate families and bestowing on him all the love they had to offer.

When World War II erupted, Lloyd, as a single parent, avoided the draft. The war created numerous job opportunities, and he began work as a security guard at the Army Ammunition Plant in nearby Charlestown, Indiana. Eventually, he rose to a supervisor's spot. The pay was good, though the hours were long, and as much as he wanted to bring Jackie back to his home, the demanding schedule prevented Lloyd from reuniting with his son under his own roof.

Not long after the war began, Lloyd began dating Bradford, Indiana native Helen Brockman, and after a brief courtship, the pair married in November 1942. They soon moved into a house at 1262 Vincennes Street and brought Jackie home as soon as possible. To Lloyd's immense relief, Helen loved the boy, and the child loved his stepmother in return.

Lloyd had a steady, well-paying job, and the future looked bright. Life was good for the little family.

On Wednesday, March 31, 1943, just four months after the marriage, Lloyd and two of his friends—twenty-eight-year-old Robert Guethe, who lived at 1916 Charlestown Road, and twenty-seven-year-old Robert McCurdy, of 2107 Willard Avenue, both in New Albany—decided to take Guethe's small boat and venture out on nearby Silver Creek for a day of fishing. They enjoyed the beautiful spring weather as they fished the cool, clear water and landed several nice specimens. They'd traveled up the creek to a point about two miles above the town of Speed, Indiana, when the boat's motor quit working.

Lloyd called his wife at about four o'clock to tell her he'd be late coming home due to the problems with the boat. She told him to be careful and that she'd see him when he got home. Lloyd went back to the boat and climbed aboard the small craft.

Guethe pulled and pulled on the small outboard, but the engine refused to fire. Exasperated, Guethe stood up to give the cord a harder yank than he could manage sitting down, and as he tugged on the starter cord, the boat overturned, tossing all three into the water. McCordy and Guethe quickly surfaced, but Lloyd didn't come up.

Guethe swam to shore and headed for help as McCord dove under the water time and again trying to find Lloyd, but his efforts proved in vain. Officers from the Indiana State Police found Sinkhorn's body two hours later. He had a small bruise on his forehead, possibly indicating that the boat had struck him and rendered him unconscious. He wore a watch that wasn't waterproof, and the timepiece had stopped at exactly four thirty.

His funeral was held at two o'clock on Saturday, April 3, 1943, in the Culbertson Avenue Baptist Church in New Albany, after which he was laid next to Ruth in the Graceland Memorial Park in Lot 86 on Hill 3. He was survived by four brothers: William, who lived in Indianapolis; Leslie, a resident of Louisville, Kentucky; and Harold and Merrill, who still lived in New Albany. Only one of his sisters, Ethel Bard of Louisville, survived him.

Described to me by her stepson, Lloyd "Jack" Sinkhorn, as a "saint," Helen never remarried, raising Jack on her own while working as the office manager of the old W.T. Grant store on the southeast corner of Spring and Pearl Streets. She died on Friday, November 6, 1998, in the Rolling Hills Healthcare Center. Her body lay in state at the Kraft Funeral Home on Spring Street from one o'clock to eight o'clock on Sunday, November 8, and her funeral was held in the Holy Family Catholic Church at eleven o'clock in the morning on Monday, November 9. Jackie Sinkhorn buried his stepmother on the other side of his father in the Kraft-Graceland Memorial Park.

Jack Sinkhorn, a former active duty officer in the United States Marine Corps, still lives in New Albany as of this writing. He and his wife, who recently celebrated their fiftieth wedding anniversary, have two boys and two girls and three grandchildren. When interviewed for this story, Jack told me that he didn't know his mother committed suicide until he was in his fifties, when he and his oldest daughter went to the Indiana Room of the New Albany–Floyd County Library and found the article in the *New Albany Tribune* about her death. The discovery didn't change the way he felt about her. He could have turned into a bitter young man due to the terrible losses he suffered at such an early age, but the kindness and love shown to him by his stepmother instead made him the caring individual he is today, thereby preventing another possible tragedy in the Sinkhorn family.

# Care to Make a Bet?

Raymond L. Jaegers loved softball. He enjoyed the sport so much that the forty-six-year-old mayor of New Albany sponsored his own team in the summer of 1946.[10] Sadly, considering his admiration of and dedication to the sport, the squad—named the Mayor Jaegers in honor of its benefactor— found itself in last place in league standings when it faced the formidable Cafemen at Bicknell Park on the night of Wednesday, July 3.

Jaegers's crew, under the management of Edwin Loebig, came out swinging, scoring a run in the first inning, but the Cafemen answered with a run of their own in the second. The mayor's players regained the lead in the third, but the Cafemen's starting pitcher, Tommy Voss, the latter making his Inter-Cities League debut that muggy summer night, held the Mayor Jaegers scoreless for the next three innings. Jay Lindsay replaced his new teammate on the mound in the top of the sixth, and the Cafemen tied the score in the bottom of the inning. The battle continued for another six innings until, in the bottom of the twelfth, the Cafemen's second baseman, Pete Murphy, beat out a slow roller for an infield single. Mayor Jaegers's starting pitcher, Red Lee, who'd only allowed six hits up to this point, purposefully walked the Cafemen's next batter, Ralph Voss, and with runners on first and second, Mike Hoffman stepped to the plate. Hoffman banged a ringing single to right center, allowing the speedy Murphy to cross home plate, giving the Cafemen the victory. Though surely not pleased with the outcome, Mayor Jaegers doubtless enjoyed the brief respite the game afforded him from his demanding schedule.

Born in New Albany on June 23, 1902, one of ten children of Edmund A. and Mary K. Jaegers, the future politician spent much of his early life working on the family's farm on Green Valley Road. Life as a farmer's son instilled a strong work ethic in the young man, a trait he valued throughout his life. He never finished school and went to work as a moulder in the Gohmann-Kahler factory. At some point during the Roaring Twenties, he met and married Virginia Huckeby. The newlyweds moved into his parents' home, and in 1929, their first child, a daughter they named Virginia Lou, arrived. Another daughter, Carolyn Ann, came along two years later, and in 1934, Virginia finally gave birth to a son, a boy the couple named after his father. The family lived on the farm where the future mayor grew up and regularly attended services at the First Baptist Church in New Albany.

Raymond continued in his position at Gohmann-Kahler until a growing interest in politics around the time his son arrived led to Jaegers's appointment as a deputy sheriff by Floyd County sheriff Oda I. Pyle on January 1, 1935. Two years later, Jaegers won Pyle's former office and served two terms as the Floyd County sheriff before winning the mayor's office in the fall of 1942. The newly elected Republican mayor resigned his position as sheriff on December 31 of that year and assumed the reins of the city the next day, January 1, 1943.

Shortly after winning the election, though hesitant to leave his widower father, he moved his family to a spacious home at 1117 East Elm Street in order to be closer to the city he now ran.

He spent much of his time in office successfully attracting new industry to New Albany, and his efforts helped land a small airport near the town. When not wooing potential businesses, Jaegers turned his attention to municipal matters, and many civil projects started during his administration. One of his pet projects was the painting and cleaning up of the city, and his interest in recreation was the driving force behind the buildup of the city's parks. The switch from streetcars to buses for public transportation occurred during his term, and during World War II, Jaegers had ground plowed up in Falling Run Park, encouraging New Albanians to cultivate victory gardens on the tilled land. He and Virginia did their part for victory, growing vegetables on a spot in the park, and the farmer's son enjoyed the time he and his wife spent tending to their little garden in the city's west end. Work began on a proposed flood control project to protect the city from ever again enduring the suffering and devastation wrought during the disastrous 1937 flood, and once the circuit court established a district, the mayor was elected to head the New Albany Board of Floodwall Commissioners.

As mayor, Jaegers also served as justice of the peace for the city. Citizens charged with minor crimes like public intoxication, disorderly conduct and other unimportant offenses appeared before him for settlement of their cases. On March 4, 1946, Jaegers presided over a minor case with major consequences. Eugene Walker, an African American New Albanian who lived at 517 State Street, had been arrested two days before on charges of carrying a concealed weapon. Chief Ben Wolfe brought the accused and the pistol, an old model .38-caliber revolver, to the mayor's office. After hearing the evidence, Jaegers fined Walker fifteen dollars and confiscated the gun. When Walker left the office, the mayor placed the pistol in one of his desk drawers, and there the handgun remained for the next six months and one day.

In addition to his responsibilities as New Albany's chief executive, Jaegers also belonged to several local fraternal organizations, among them the Optimist Club, the Chamber of Commerce, the Floyd County Berry Growers Association, the Floyd County Coon Hunters Association, the Floyd County Conservation Club, the Red Cross, the Jefferson Lodge 104 of the Free Masons, the Travelers Protective Association, the Parent-Teacher Association and the International Moulders and Foundry Workers of America. In 1945, he served as the director of third-class cities[11] on the executive board of the Indiana Municipal League, and on July 26, 1946, he became the first New Albany mayor ever appointed to higher office of the association when elected first vice-president of the group.

Mayor Raymond L. Jaegers was indeed a busy man when he accepted the vice-presidency of the municipal league, but the extra time he'd need to properly attend to his new office was the least of his troubles that summer. Along with the normal problems and headaches associated with his position as chief executive of the city, Jaegers had recently become embroiled in a dispute with the local labor union representing the city's police and firefighters. Though organized labor had been a major supporter of the mayor in the last election, the department's union representatives had requested pay raises for their organizations that Jaegers considered excessive. The conflict threatened the relationship with labor he knew he'd need again in his next campaign, but in a move almost unheard-of in this era of self-serving politicians, his sense of duty and responsibility to the people of New Albany overrode his personal concerns, and he refused to present the issue to the city council. However, the repudiation of the request created even bigger troubles for the honorable politician than the loss of the union's support in the coming elections.

In early August, just a little over a month after his team lost to the Cafemen, a group of concerned New Albanians, including Paul Schultz, president of the Junior Chamber of Commerce, Reverend Theodore Tiemeyer of the New Albany Ministerial Association, Mrs. C.V. Rodman and Mrs. C.E. Fleming of the Parent-Teacher Association and William E. Rogers of the East End Civic Club formed the New Albany Better Government

Committee. The group, led by Dudley Jewell, executive director of the New Albany Chamber of Commerce, vowed "vigorous action" if city officials didn't address within two weeks the large-scale gambling in New Albany, a situation they described as a "booming business" "unmolested" by the town's authorities.

The mayor believed the dispute between his office and the labor union played a large part in the formation of the organization, and while Jaegers and his supporters may have been correct in the assumption about the motivation behind the formation of the anti-gambling crusade, the committee was correct on at least two counts: the size of the problem and the local authority's hands-off approach to the crime.

Though throughout the city's history the occasional crackdowns on gambling had occurred, illegal wagering had always been a big, albeit semi-underground, activity in New Albany. Many of the town's fraternal organizations had (and may still have) slot machines hidden away in the back rooms of their buildings, and one could/can generally find a card or dice game going on in the hidden enclaves as well. Most of the organizations used/use the money earned from the illicit goings-on to support their philanthropic actions on behalf of the community, and most New Albanians generally had/have no problem with the fraternal gaming. When a riverboat casino opened in the 1990s a little over twelve miles down the river and just across the Floyd/Harrison border (an operation that was initially offered to New Albany and was, in light of city's gambling past, surprisingly voted down…twice), some of the illegal activity ceased, but if one wants to find a card or dice game, or place a bet on a horse race or sporting event, a word in the right ear will quickly lead you to someone willing to accept the wager.

On August 20, Chief Wolfe issued a statement in which he declared that the police department would soon take matters into its own hands to guarantee enforcement of the laws against gambling in the city. At noon on Tuesday, August 21, in response to the charge that members of the department received graft from the gambling consortium, the police put the gaming houses on notice. A spokesman for the department warned that all suspected organized gambling houses would be watched twenty-four hours a day for any illicit activity. The police representative further claimed that the action had nothing to do with the failure of the city council to act on the requested wage increases; the timing of the ban was a simple coincidence.

The gamblers heeded the warning; at least, they did that night. The next day, the *New Albany Tribune* reported that "all the gambling houses were dark and quiet." Jaegers told the paper he had "no comment to make on the action of the police department," which action had been done without the department informing the mayor or seeking his approval.

Within a few days, the police began a series of gambling raids—again, without informing the city's chief executive or getting his consent prior to the searches. The forays angered Jaegers, but Wolfe repeated the department's assertion that the raids were meant to counter claims that the local gambling consortium paid the police to ignore them. Despite the department's repeated denials of any wrongdoing, the claims against it were probably true.

On August 23, the mayor met with members of the anti-gambling committee. He claimed the actions of his police chief "hurt" his feelings and that the police "jumped the gun" by beginning the crackdown before he could issue an order for the department to put a halt to the illegal activity. Jaegers claimed in the meeting that "the lid on gambling in this city will be clamped on firmly. Bingo, slot machines in private clubs, and every other form of gaming must go." He then turned to Wolfe and ordered his chief to see that "gambling everywhere and in all forms should be wiped out in New Albany." Then, in an attempt to prove his determination to stop the illicit wagering, Jaegers threatened to fire the entire police force if his order to end gambling in the city was not immediately put into action.

The next day, on August 24, in response to the mayor's threat to fire the police officers, a representative for the department told a reporter for the *Louisville Courier Journal*, "We have stopped public gambling before the mayor ever opened his mouth." The bickering, and the crackdown, continued, and on August 27, stress generated by the conflict between law enforcement and his office, in combination with all of his numerous obligations, proved too much for the diabetic Jaegers. His private physician, Dr. William C. Winstandley, claiming Jaegers was "overworked, run down, and on the verge of a nervous breakdown," confined the mayor to his bed indefinitely. Following the doctor's orders, the mayor took to his bed. On Wednesday, September 4, a reporter for the *New Albany Tribune* visited Jaegers at his home. The journalist claimed that the "downcast and moody" mayor, whom he thought did not look well, said he felt "so weak that he was thinking of staying home for several days longer."

Despite the mayor's alleged statement to the reporter that Wednesday morning, that afternoon he spent a couple hours in his office. The next morning, Thursday, September 5, 1946, Jaegers rose early. According to his family, he appeared cheerful and looked forward to returning to his office later that morning. He seemed eager to wade into the stack of work he knew had piled up on his desk in his absence. Before going to the courthouse on the southeast corner of Spring and State Streets, he and his wife went to their little garden plot in Falling Run Park to pick beans, which Mrs. Jaegers intended on canning later that day. They joked about who would pick the most beans, and Jaegers ended up picking more than her. About 8:30 a.m., the pair said goodbye, and the mayor headed for his office.

He arrived there about thirty minutes later. About twenty minutes after his arrival, he spoke with Chief Wolfe. Wolfe asked the mayor how he felt, and Jaegers responded that he felt a little better and a little stronger. Wolfe then asked if he could bring a public intoxication up to the mayor's second-floor office to be tried, and when Jaegers responded, "Yes. Bring him up," the chief headed to the jail to retrieve the accused prisoner.

Before heading into his office, Jaegers spoke with his secretary, Miss Doris Million, in her office adjoining the mayor's. They discussed several matters that needed his attention, and when finished dealing with the most pressing, Jaegers asked, "Is there anything else important to take care of?" When Million told him no, the mayor smiled and went into his office. She heard him lock the door as she turned her attention to a warrant on her desk. The mayor often locked his office door when he didn't want to be bothered while devoting his attention to some matter, and Million didn't think anything strange about him doing so that morning.

At 9:45 a.m., as she completed the form, she heard a gunshot ring out. Though the noise startled her, the loud pop didn't particularly alarm her. The secretary thought someone must have been practicing on the firing range in the basement of the building. The acoustics in the massive old structure often made it hard to pinpoint the exact location of sounds reverberating within the building's stone walls.

City clerk James Ferrell and his assistant, Mrs. Bonnie Landis, in their offices on the first floor beneath the mayor's, also heard the shot. They thought the noise came from someone practicing on the firing range, too, but were a bit more surprised at the sound than the mayor's secretary, as someone usually notified them before anyone used the range. Ferrell went in search of Chief Wolfe and asked him if he knew of anyone shooting in the basement. Wolfe told him as far as he knew, no one was down there, and when Ferrell told him about the shot, the chief, accompanied by patrolman William Flannigan, went to investigate.

When Miss Million finished with the document, she buzzed the mayor on the intercom. She needed his signature on the warrant, and when he didn't answer her electronic summons, she rapped on his door but got no answer. As she stood there wondering why her boss didn't answer her knock, Wolfe and Flannigan entered the office. They, too, knocked on the door, calling out to Jaegers, and when they got no response, they attempted to force entry to the office. Unable to break through the massive wood door, they removed the hinges and entered the mayor's office.

Jaegers sat in his chair behind his desk, his head resting against the wall. Blood covered the desk and floor around him. In his right hand, he still held the 38.-caliber revolver he'd confiscated from Eugene Walker exactly six months and one day prior to that fateful morning when New Albany's mayor Raymond L. Jaegers ended his own life.

Wolfe notified the police and fire departments of the incident and then notified the Floyd County coroner, Dr. Frank T. Tyler. Word quickly spread throughout the town, and the coroner had to push through the milling crowd gathered in front of the courthouse. Upon entering the mayor's office, Tyler examined the body before surveying the room. He questioned Miss Million, Chief Wolfe and Officer Flannigan about the circumstances immediately preceding their unpleasant discovery and then asked Chief Wolfe, "Well, is it suicide or murder?" Wolfe said he didn't think it possible that the death could be anything but suicide, and the other two witnesses agreed with the chief's opinion. Accordingly, Tyler's verdict reflected that belief. Jaeger's body was taken to the Mullineaux Funeral Home and prepared for burial.

Virginia Jaegers sat on the front porch of her home stringing the beans she and her husband had picked earlier that sunny summer morning when she noticed New Albany fire chief George Hanen pull up in front of the house. She briefly wondered why Hanen was there but cheerfully greeted the family friend, her pleasure quickly turning to shock and horror when the chief delivered the dreadful news of her beloved husband's demise. Hanen later said he thought his friend was going to faint, stating, "She didn't say much before she began sobbing." Gathering her wits about her, Virginia asked where her husband's body was and then asked that her children be gathered from their respective schools and brought to the family's residence. She asked that they not be told the reason for the unexpected reprieve from school.

UNFORTUNATELY, MAYOR JAEGER'S suicide was not New Albany's only noteworthy event to occur that fateful September day.

As Dudley Jewell, executive director of the New Albany Chamber of Commerce and head of the anti-gambling coalition, sat in his office in the chamber's headquarters on the southeast corner of Bank and Spring Streets a little after one o'clock that auspicious afternoon, he heard his secretary, Mrs. Velma Shacklette, arguing with a man in her office. A few seconds later, an obviously angry James Stocksdale stormed into the director's office.

Stocksdale, a career criminal with a lengthy record, had been arrested numerous times on a variety of charges including public intoxication, disorderly conduct, destroying private property, trespassing, malicious trespassing, assault and battery, petite and grand larceny, auto theft and robbery. His crimes had cost him hundreds of dollars in fines and restitution, and he'd spent a large part of his adult life locked up behind bars. Though currently under a suspended sentence for cutting another man in June, and despite his rather disreputable past, Stocksdale was, almost unbelievably, the Democratic candidate for New Albany city constable. He also allegedly ran the blackjack and dice games found throughout the city.

"I'm going to get you for the part you played in stopping the gambling," the criminal constable candidate raged at Jewell.

"What are you talking about?" the director asked.

"Why did you shut down my dice games?" Stocksdale demanded.

"I don't know what you're talking about."

"Yes, you do. You and that damned committee."

"The police closed your games. Not me."

"You're taking food out of my kids' mouths. Are you going to do something about this?"

"There's nothing I can do."

Stocksdale pulled a knife from his pocket. "I'm gonna ask you one more time. Are you gonna do anything or not?"

"No."

Stocksdale then leapt at Jewell, slashing at him with the knife. The blade cut a deep, five-inch gash on the director's left cheek. Jewell miraculously avoided two or three more swipes of the razor-sharp dagger and fled through his office door with Stocksdale in close pursuit. Jewell's secretary sat in stunned amazement for a few moments, then called the police and reported the attack.

Stocksdale chased his intended victim out into the street. When Jewell ran into the office of Dr. John Parris, located across the street from the chamber's headquarters, Stocksdale abandoned the pursuit and headed west on Spring Street. Minutes later, the police arrested him as he casually strolled down the street. They took him to the county lockup and charged Stocksdale with assault and battery with intent to kill.

Jewell was taken to St. Edward's Hospital on Spring Street and treated for his injury. He was released on Saturday afternoon, September 7. The cut left a large scar, which he carried as a reminder of that notorious afternoon for the rest of his life.

DESPITE THE UPROAR in the city created by the mayor's suicide and the attack on Jewell, the police crackdown on gambling continued in the city. Just ten hours after Jaegers killed himself, the police raided seven suspected gambling houses. The officers seized telephones, headphones, loudspeakers, racing slips and blackboards—all the things one could expect to find in any gaming establishment. The raiders arrested seven individuals, charging the prisoners with unlawfully keeping a building for gaming purposes. Those arrested and the purported establishments where the gambling occurred were:

Dennis Burke, 1624 East Market Street
Robert "Shorty" Gonder, 418 Vincennes Street
Clarence Jamison, 226 State Street
Claude McBride and Harry and Russell Daniels, Daniels Café
114 East Market Street
Courtney Snider, 311 Vincennes Street
James R. Hukill, 238 Vincennes Street

During the raid at Hukill's place, the angry gambler tried to destroy the warrant and ended up in a losing battle with New Albany police officer Harry Mason. Hukill's wife struck Officer Mason with a rolled-up newspaper, then tried to grab the patrolman's gun. Mason warned the woman to "Get away!" and called for assistance. His partner, patrolman Edward Tuft, grabbed the feisty Mrs. Hukill, and the husband and wife soon found themselves in handcuffs and headed for the county lockup, both charged with disorderly conduct and resisting arrest in addition to the charges of illegal gaming.

The accused faced arraignment on Friday morning before Floyd County judge D. Kirke Hedden. Prior to the arraignment, Hedden indicated that he wanted bond set at $1,000, but Floyd County prosecutor Nicholas Leist said he thought $500 would be more reasonable, and Judge Hedden agreed. The defendants all pleaded not guilty and headed straight to the sheriff's office immediately after the arraignment to post their bail. Chester Graf posted bond for the Daniels brothers.

Stocksdale waived arraignment in the Floyd County Circuit Court that same morning and was placed under a $3,500 bail, his trial set for sometime in October. He returned to his cell in the county jail, and there he would remain until his trial. No one would post his bail.

That afternoon, the city council appointed one of its members, E.K. Scott, as mayor pro tem until the following Thursday when the council expected to name a new mayor. At the time of his appointment, Scott informed the council that he had no desire to remain in the position permanently. Who could blame him?

The council began a search for a new mayor, and when asked by a *Tribune* reporter what type of man it was looking for to serve as mayor, a spokesman for the group claimed, "The council wants a type of man who will give the city the kind of administration every good citizen has a right to expect."

The two incidents that black Thursday drew the attention of news organizations from across the country, and several reporters from around the nation descended on the city, making their headquarters in the offices of the *New Albany Tribune*. A reporter from Indianapolis interviewed Stocksdale in his cell on Friday morning. When asked why he'd attacked Jewell, the prisoner responded:

*Because he was destroying my way of making a living. That's why I was running for constable—to add a little to my income. Hell, I've got three kids I have to feed. Gambling's all I can do. They won't let me have no other work. I've always run an honest game—mostly blackjack and dice. I never let nobody ever leave my place broke, even if I have to give 'em a buck or two. That's the way I earn my living and that guy was trying to take my living away from me. I've got as much right to earn a living as he has. He don't give a damn about my kids.*

Stocksdale languished in the county jail, but even behind bars he still caused trouble in New Albany. Though he'd resigned his candidacy the evening of his arrest, the head of the Floyd County Election Board, former Floyd County sheriff and then Floyd County clerk Oda L. Pyle, the sheriff who'd given Jaegers his job as a deputy sheriff, wasn't sure Stocksdale *could* resign.

Pyle, a Republican, called the state election board on Friday afternoon for clarification. He received an answer on Saturday from board member Edwin Steers Sr., who would serve as one of Indiana's at-large alternate delegates to the Republican National Convention in 1952, claimed:

*Section 114 of the state election code says, "If any candidate whose nomination has been certified according to law shall wish to resign from such ticket, he shall file his resignation in writing with the county election officer before August 1."*

*From the above it can be seen that a candidate is prohibited from resigning after August 1. We know of no provision in the law for the removal of a candidate after that date.*

As far as the state election board was concerned, the incarcerated candidate, who'd won the nomination with 1,132 votes in the May primary, would remain the Democratic nominee for city constable.

The board's response outraged the Floyd County Democratic Party. Paul Tegart, chairman of the party, believed the Republican's actions were an attempt to sully the reputation of the Democratic Party in Floyd County. Tegart stated, "I'm going to exhaust every legal possibility to see that the name of Stocksdale is removed from the Democratic ticket." Tegart further claimed that if successful in the attempt, he'd either name another candidate to the position or leave the spot blank.

Pyle responded to the Democrat's accusation that partisan politics drove his actions:

> *Politics are not a factor in my decision to let the name of Stocksdale remain on the Democratic ballot. I'm acting fair and square and according to the law. If the Democrats knew the police record of the man they should not have elected him to be their party's candidate for Constable in the May primary.*

While the political parties battled and the police waged war against the gamblers, Jaegers's funeral, a "brief and quiet" affair amid all of the city's turmoil, took place at two thirty that Saturday afternoon in the chapel of Mullineaux's funeral home. Reverend Harry M. Davis, pastor of the Central Christian Church, conducted the service, and a score of mayors from cities all over Indiana, as well as Indiana's secretary of state, A.B. Burch, and the Indiana Municipal League, sent telegrams of condolence and floral arrangements. The huge number of floral memorials banked from floor to ceiling along all four walls of one room in the funeral home.

More than nine hundred people signed the registration book while the mayor's body lay in state in an open coffin. Among those in attendance during the service were the executive secretary of the state municipal league, Crown Point, Indiana mayor W.V. Yonkey, and Bloomington, Indiana mayor Loba Jack Bruner, a director of the league and a past president of the organization. Louisville, Kentucky mayor E. Leland Taylor attended, but Jeffersonville mayor Sam Shannon couldn't be there due to a previous commitment to attend another funeral taking place at the same time as Jaegers's service. Quartermaster Sergeant Bruce McAllister, a member of the Sixteenth Infantry Battalion of the United States Marine Corps and an old schoolmate of Jaegers, made an unexpected visit to the service. Edwin Loebig, manager of the Mayor Jaegers, also attended the funeral. Later that evening, in honor of their former benefactor, Loebig announced the cancellation of the team's game against the New Albany Grays, scheduled for Sunday afternoon in Bicknell Park.

The honorary pallbearers included members of the city council, Judge D. Kirke Hedden, City Clerk Ferrell, New Albany Township assessor William

A. Beach, city engineer Ad Jackson, Robert Kelso and Kenneth Hardin. Chief Wolfe, Chief Hanen, assistant fire chiefs William Kelley and Virgil Owens, city auditor John Peters, welfare director James Stucker, city attorney Evan McLinn and county clerk Oda Pyle served as the actual pallbearers. Jaegers's friends carried him to the Fairview Cemetery and, after a brief service at the graveside, bid him a final goodbye before returning to their respective homes. Mayor Raymond L. Jaegers ended up in Plot 5, Range 2, Lot 14, Grave 6, in the Fairview Cemetery…but not that afternoon. At the request of the mayor's widow and her father, J. W.M. "Willy" Huckeby, his body went back to Mullineaux's.

Rumors quickly spread through New Albany that the mayor hadn't died by his own hand. Some claimed Jaegers met his death at the murderous hands of a local representative of the gambling consortium in the city. The gamers reputedly had ties to nationally organized crime syndicates, and other New Albanians believed their mayor's death was a professional hit by a mob killer. The family heard the wild tales, and the grieving widow and her father asked for a paraffin wax test done on the dead man's hands to determine if he had indeed fired the gun that supposedly killed him, followed by an autopsy.

Mrs. Jaegers and her father claimed Jaegers had been in a cheerful mood when they last saw him that fateful morning, more jovial than he'd been in days, and all of the family members, when asked, said he'd been particularly happy about returning to his office. Mrs. Jaegers and her father said that Wolfe and Miss Million told them that nothing unpleasant occurred during their discussions with the mayor in the minutes prior to his supposed suicide, and no one had come forward with information about any other events that could possibly account for the change in their loved one's disposition from cheerful to so desperate he felt he had nothing to live for in such a short amount of time.

"We feel that there is a distinct possibility that Raymond did not commit suicide," his father-in-law told a *Tribune* reporter. "Of course, I am not a detective, but I hope the city and state police will sift this thing to the bottom."

When the reporter asked if the family had any idea who might have wanted to harm his son-in-law, Huckeby responded, "No. We have no clues and hold no one under suspicion. It is simply that if Raymond did not kill himself—and we are positive he did not—then his slayer should be found and brought to justice."

The journalist then asked Mrs. Jaegers if any threats had ever been made against her husband's life. She said she didn't know of any, then added, "But he wouldn't have mentioned them if any had been made for fear of worrying me."

Coroner Tyler, in response to the reporter's questions about the family's request, stated, "Of course, when Mrs. Jaegers and Mr. Huckeby requested the autopsy, I agreed, because I want everyone to be convinced my verdict is correct."

I bet he did—though probably not for the reasons he publicly professed.

"If there is the slightest possibility that Jaegers met with foul play, no stone should be left unturned to determine that fact," Tyler insisted. "However, I can see no such possibility."

I don't know if his sentence referred to the possibility of foul play…or the stone turning.

Chief Wolfe gave his consent, and officers from the Indiana State Police trained in the science of forensics waited in the preparation room of the funeral home for the mayor's return. Though forensics then was not what it is today, the officers at least had enough training and experience to make a more thorough examination than anyone in New Albany. The state police first looked at the area around the entry wound near his temple. The examination showed powder burns indicating that the shot that killed Jaegers had come from almost point-blank range. The police then conducted the requested paraffin test on the hand in which Jaegers held the pistol when found.

The test is done by applying a coat of melted paraffin to the back of the individual's hand. Once the wax cools and hardens, the cast is removed and coated with certain chemicals that react to the presence of any firearm residue. According to James Smythe Wallace, in his book *Chemical Analysis of Firearms, Ammunition, and Gunshot Residue*, investigators first used paraffin wax in 1914 as a lifting medium for propellant residue on clothing prior to a chemical test to determine if the cloth held any gunpowder residue. In 1933, the analysis was successfully tested on the hand of someone who had recently fired a pistol.

In 1935, the Federal Bureau of Investigation claimed the test was not specific and that several common substances, such as tobacco, fertilizers, certain paints and even urine could produce a false positive result. The bureau's reservations revolved around its concern false positives could wrongly convict someone of a shooting—not because it had any worries about the test giving false negative results.

After conducting their analysis, the state police experts found no trace of gunpowder residue in or on the skin of the mayor's hand that held the alleged suicide weapon. Mrs. Jaegers then requested an autopsy be immediately performed. She later explained her reason for the postmortem examination to a reporter for the *New Albany Tribune*:

> *From the very first I did not believe Raymond fired the gun that killed him. So I requested a paraffin test made of his hand to determine if he had fired the gun. I have been informed that such a test is reliable even after embalming. If the test proved that he did fire the gun or if there was a reasonable doubt, I would have dropped the matter, and would not have asked for the autopsy. But since I am assured that the test proved negative, I want everything possible done to prove the case one way or the other.*

Dr. Parvin Davis conducted the autopsy that afternoon in the preparation room at Mullineaux's. Davis opened Jaegers's shattered skull and removed the bullet that killed the mayor. Unfortunately, the state police officers found the projectile badly distorted from contact with the skull opposite the point where the slug entered Jaegers's temple. They expressed doubt as to whether or not ballistic and other tests would prove conclusive. The state police took the deformed bullet and gun to their laboratory in Indianapolis that afternoon. Before they left, Tyler provided the officers with another bullet from the gun that had allegedly killed Jaegers.

Two days later, on Tuesday, September 10, the state police reported that though the slug removed from Jaegers's shattered skull was too mutilated to determine if the projectile had been fired from the pistol found in the mayor's lifeless hand, their ballistics experts believed the weapon was indeed the one that had killed him. Unbelievably, they based their verdict on one fact: that both the bullet given them by Tyler and the one removed from Jaegers had been propelled by black powder.

A disappointed Mrs. Jaegers told the *Tribune*, "We had so hoped that we could clear our minds for all time whether my husband was assassinated or committed suicide." She planned to let the matter rest in the hands of the police chief, a man she claimed "has always been a trustworthy friend. If any further action is to be taken it will be up to Police Chief Ben H. Wolfe." Chief Wolfe planned no further action in the investigation unless some other information appeared that showed the death wasn't a suicide. Tyler's judgment would stand, and the official verdict remains to this day that Mayor Raymond L. Jaegers committed suicide in his office.

Meanwhile, the battle over Stocksdale's candidacy continued. The Democrats' head honcho, Tegart, planned to put stickers over Stocksdale's name on the ballots, claiming the action was in accordance with a state law that stated:

> *Except as provided in section 234 concerning vacancies as applied to war ballots, in case of death, removal, or resignation of any candidate after the printing of such ballots and before such election, it shall be lawful for the chairman of the county political organization of which such candidate was a member to make a nomination to fill such vacancy, and to provide the election board of each precinct in which such candidate is to be voted for with a number of pasters containing only the name of such candidate at least equal to the number of ballots provided each precinct, and it shall be the duty of the precinct election clerks to put one of such pasters in a careful and proper manner and in the proper place on each ticket.*

John Peters, chairman of the Floyd County GOP, protested to the state election board regarding Tegart's attempt, and on the day Mrs. Jaegers determined to place her trust in Chief Wolfe, the board claimed that the law Tegart planned to use to remove Stocksdale from the ballots applied only to war ballots printed before August 1 and not to any other ballots used in the general election. Stocksdale remained the Democratic Party's candidate.

Jaegers's secretary, Miss Million, told his widow she'd clean out the mayor's office and send his belongings to the Jaegers home. Mrs. Jaegers gratefully accepted the offer, and on Wednesday, September 11, as Million went about her task, she emptied the contents of a drawer from the deceased mayor's desk on top of the piece of furniture. Among the pile of miscellaneous papers, one small slip of paper caught her eye. Thinking the piece a receipt of some sort, Million read the writing on the paper:

*Dear Art,*
*Take care of the children.*
*Virginia, love, I can't take it anymore.*
*Ray*

The stunned secretary turned the paper over, and on the back of the two-inch-wide slip, she saw more writing: "I thought I had friends, but C.V. Lorch, James Montgomery, and Jewell is [*sic*] the cause of my death."

No signature accompanied the words, which Million believed to be in her former boss's handwriting. Chief Wolfe, Clerk Ferrell, Coroner Tyler and Judge Hedden agreed with the secretary's assessment.

Former Floyd County prosecutor Chester V. Lorch, a sergeant in the famed Rainbow Division during World War I, had served briefly as the city's Republican mayor after the death of Republican mayor Noble Mitchell in 1942 before resigning his office to serve his country as a colonel in the Army Air Corps. His departure led to Jaegers's election. After the war, Lorch rejoined his brother Frank in the successful law firm the pair had established in New Albany in 1928.[12]

Montgomery, publisher of the *New Albany Tribune*, who was out of town when Million found the purported suicide note, made no public response to the contents of the brief message, but Jewell and Lorch expressed surprise at the comments. Jewell, recuperating at home, responded to the remarks blaming him for the suicide: "Mayor Jaegers' death came as a stunning blow to me. I have lost a close friend—the community has lost a progressive leader. In his confusion and illness he has placed the responsibility for his death in error."

Apparently, no one found it strange enough to comment publicly that the mayor wrote the purported suicide note on such a small scrap of paper, especially with plenty of paper available in his or his secretary's office. Nor did anyone publicly question why he would have stuck his explanation away amidst a pile of other papers in his desk drawer. Maybe they feared they'd meet the same fate as their chief executive.

The facts surrounding Jaegers's death remain unclear, but one thing was crystal clear: the city needed a new mayor, and on September 14, the *Tribune* announced that former mayor C. Robert Brooks was expected to be appointed as New Albany's new chief by the city council. Brooks had been appointed mayor by the council in June 1942 upon Lorch's departure for the Air Corps and held the position until Jaegers assumed office on January 1, 1943. But despite the paper's assertion, Brooks, owner of a successful real estate agency, refused the council's offer, claiming his business required so much of his attention that he'd only be able to spend a couple of hours each day in the chief executive's seat. The search continued.

On Thursday morning, September 19, Stocksdale surprised everyone by pleading guilty to the charges against him. Judge Hedden immediately imposed sentence. Stocksdale was to be imprisoned in the state penitentiary in Michigan City, Indiana, for a period of between one to ten years, the maximum penalty the judge could impose. Stocksdale entered the plea without representation. Apparently, not even a lawyer wanted any type of association with the man. The career criminal was taken away that afternoon.

Thursday night, the city council named fifty-four-year-old World War I veteran J. Irvin Streepey, manager of the D.F. Bowman Waste Company since 1926, New Albany's newest mayor. Council member Joe A. Binford made the nomination, the only one offered. Streepey, a graduate of New Albany High School and the Jefferson School of Law in Louisville, Kentucky, became the city's seventh mayor in eight years when he assumed the office that night.

The new mayor, a widower, lived at 1239 Beechwood Avenue and had two sons, Dr. J. I. Streepey and Robert, who was then attending the dental school at the University of Louisville. Streepey kept as busy a schedule as his predecessor. After the swearing-in ceremony, the new mayor said, "I shall meet issues as they arise. Since I am not a candidate for this office, I have no program or platform." He then asked for the support of the citizens of New Albany to help make the city a better place in which to live. He then indicated he would make a further statement on city policies in the next few days.

Montgomery commented on the event on the front page of his paper the next day:

> *The members of the New Albany city council are to be congratulated not only for selecting an outstanding citizen as mayor but for persuading him to take the helm and guide the city in difficult times.*
>
> *The unfortunate and tragic train of events which culminated in the necessity of selecting a new mayor are much to be regretted. The fact the one man "gave up" when faced with problems which he must have felt were*

*too complex for him to solve, is ample proof of the trying job which Mayor J. Irvin Streepey now courageously undertakes.*

*We believe most folks in New Albany share with* The Tribune *a confidence that the Streepey administration will be one of benefit to the city. We do not expect the impossible. We do not expect every act of Mayor Streepey will be entirely pleasing to us or to you of New Albany's citizenry. But we feel strongly that he will attempt to do a conscious job to the best of his high ability.*

*Some of us may not like all the laws he and we are bound by but we must keep in mind that we all had a greater part in their making than did the new mayor and that, in asking him to do a job, we have delegated him to do OUR job under OUR laws.*

*Even though being a mayor of New Albany is not necessarily a full-time job, any competent man must make sacrifices to do it well. We do not know what mayor Streepey expects to do about city employees who serve under his appointment and direction, but we can guess that he will try to get the worth of your dollars spent for their services. That's what we should expect of all public servants.*

*Remember that the mayor has been employed to work for you. Give him a hand and help him do the good job you and he want done.*

When the new mayor entered his office the next morning at eleven o'clock, a basket of red roses from the Mutual Trust and Deposit Company greeted him. If his comments constituted a veiled threat to the gambling syndicate, they went unheeded. Gambling remained an issue in the city for years afterward.

Almost unbelievably, in November, inmate Stocksdale won his race. The Democratic candidate received 3,811 votes. As can be expected, he didn't serve a day as constable.

Obviously, we can never truly account for the actions of someone whose mental state is deranged enough to lead him to suicide, but nothing in Jaegers's actions preceding his demise would lead anyone to believe him insane. The only thing he did that might cause us to question his sanity was his final act, but in September 1946, many New Albanians didn't believe their mayor had killed himself. Many contemporary citizens of the city still don't, including this author.

Care to make a bet?

# Notes

## Introduction

1. As of this writing, David Camm has stood trial for the murders of his wife and children—twice. Both convictions have been overturned by the Indiana Court of Appeals. Camm is still in prison and awaiting a decision on whether he will face a third trial for his part in the murders. In February 2006, another man, Charles Darnell Boney, (pronounced Bo-Neh), was convicted of murder and conspiracy to commit murder in connection with the deaths of Kim, Jill and Brad. Boney is currently serving 225 years for his part in their deaths.

## Murder Most Foul

2. This figure does not include victims of arson for some reason.

3. In January 2010, one week before he was scheduled to go to trial for the murder, Love was found not competent to stand trial and was taken to the Logansport, Indiana state hospital. As of this writing, Love remains in the institution and has yet to face the consequences of his act.

4. Less than five months later, in the early morning hours of December 12, Sheriff Fullenlove would be shot in the arm and severely wounded when a band of approximately one hundred vigilantes from Seymour, Indiana,

descended on New Albany, forced their way into the jail and hanged three of the infamous Reno brothers from beams inside the lockup. Fullenlove was beaten and shot when he refused to hand over the keys to the cells containing the notorious train robbers, and when threatened with death if he didn't, the sheriff replied, "I'll surrender my life, but not my trust."

5. The couple, married June 23, 1863, had a son they named Albert Jr., but the child died in infancy.

6. Francis married William E. Russell in September 1901, but less than a year and a half later, in early December 1902, William died.

## The Steel Wheels of Death

7. After more than fifty years of providing New Albany's hungry citizens with delicious food at reasonable prices, the restaurant closed in early February 2011.

## Suicides

8. Today, Sycamore Street is known as Culbertson Avenue.

9. As of this writing, though not a native of New Albany, Indiana University Southeast graduate and former baseball player Cameron Conner is currently playing in the minor leagues as he waits for his call to "The Show."

10. In addition to his sponsorship of the softball team, he also subsidized a regular baseball team, managed by Dan Lopp, in one of the city's leagues.

11. New Albany was made a first-class city in 1948 and has kept the ranking ever since.

12. The law firm, now known as "Lorch and Naville," still represents New Albany's citizens from its offices at 506 State Street in the city.

# About the Author

B orn in the Floyd Memorial Hospital in New Albany on July 21, 1960, Gregg Seidl has spent most of his life in the city. A 1978 graduate of New Albany High School, Seidl enlisted in the Marine Corps and was honorably discharged in August 1982. He worked for more than eighteen years in the construction industry before attending Indiana University Southeast in the fall of 2001 with his daughter, Amelia, at his side. Graduating from the college in 2006 with a bachelor of arts degree in American history, Seidl has since worked as a college instructor and substitute teacher for the Jefferson County Public School system in nearby Louisville, Kentucky. This is his second published work, and he and his wife, Corine, a sixth grade middle school English teacher, live in New Albany's east end with their cat, Moby.

Visit us at
www.historypress.net